RESONATION

ENLIGHTENED GOVERNMENT FOR WE THE PEOPLE

Gregory Olinyk

Morgan James Publishing • New York

ResoNation

ISBN: 1-60037-135-3 (Hardcover)
ISBN: 1-60037-136-1 (Paperback)
ISBN: 1-60037-137-X (Audio)

Published by:

MORGAN · JAMES
THE ENTREPRENEURIAL PUBLISHER™
www.morganjamespublishing.com

Morgan James Publishing, LLC
1225 Franklin Ave Ste 325
Garden City, NY 11530-1693
Toll Free 800-485-4943
www.MorganJamesPublishing.com

Habitat for Humanity®
Peninsula
Building Partner

General Editor:
Heather Campbell

Cover & Interior Design by:
3 Dog Design
www.3dogdesign.net
chris@3dogdesign.net

CONTENTS

ACKNOWLEDGEMENTS

In the order their appearance in the life of this book, I give thanks to my parents, Harry and Gloria, for their unselfish love to 6 kids and too many good lessons to recount here – especially about speaking up and never quitting; to my son, Oliver, who encouraged me to press on through 4 years of research, interviewing, and writing; to my brother Mark who personifies the meaning of unselfish civic service; to my boyhood friend, Michael Frank, whose warm phone calls and moral support carried me through countless rough patches during the writing process; to Dee Dee Olinyk and my daughter, Shae, who have been so supportive over the past 30 years; to Trish Waltz one of my heroes on so many levels; to Eolake Stobblehouse for his trust and belief in me and the DayLight mission that you will read about here; to Rosemary Morretta for her wise counsel and constant accessibility throughout the editing process; to Nicco Mele, Larry Biddle and Harish Rao, premier Internet political strategists who were able to appreciate the DayLight Movement concept in its early, "raw," phase; to my fearless editor, Ali Morretta, for her patience with a disorganized writer – I could not have attracted a publisher and so many supporters without her expert wordsmithing and editorial insights; to Linda Howarth and Colleen Farmer for their insights about what is important to women with regard to equality and control of their bodies; to Chuck Scott at Avanti Group for his ongoing effervescent imagination and positive input whether he agreed with a particular subject point or not; to media investment banking expert, Cliff Gardiner, for invaluable radio industry insights; to Doug Isaacson for taking calls about a wide horizon of publishing, editing and promotional concepts; to Sol Slotnik, David Albin, and Professor Michael Botein for legal and ethical advice over many years; to David and Nancy Finnie, Dr. David and Dr. Charlotte Brown and Kevork Toroyan for their Middle East and peace-oriented experience and insights; to Steve Wiggins for always seeming to know just that little bit extra that helps tell a story better and more informatively; to former Colorado Governor (now Professor) Richard D. Lamm for his insights into the immigration issue and his leadership-by-example over 4 decades of public and academic service; to John Wolfe, Dr. Jerry Capoot, Richard Stubbs, Charlie Pugh, Bradley

Panos, Phil Lowery, Don Merrill, Bradley Murdock, Russ Jones, Bill Johnson, Barry Bassett, Earl and Katherine Stewart, Chris Bent, AJ Robbins, Luis Roldan, Carl Gambello, Dr. Don Zalucky; Dr. Basil Papaharis; Jon and Nancy Dahlin, John and Renee Hanning, Herb and Madonna Duval, Scott and Carol Peterson, Peter and Paul Hershorn, Ed and Bree Robin, Dan Scouler, Tom Lycan, Pat Codute, Virginia and Jonas Olmsted, and Doug Greenwood and his team of venture "angels," all for boosting me over some formidable mission hurdles across the span of years; to Claudio Ballard, Joseph Avellino, Peter Langenus, Norman Hansen and Anand "Andy" Krishna for their encouragement to keep plugging away; to Lloyd V. Schrum a teacher whose belief in a young teenager has carried me over some high mountains in the ensuing years; to Morgan James Publishing for their wisdom, guidance and patience throughout the creation of this book; and to human-potential authors (and wise guides) Elizabeth Rann Arrott and Michael Rann for appearing at just the right time in *ResoNation's* developmental process.

Resonance:

The reinforcement and prolongation of a sound by reflection or by vibration of other adjacent bodies.

Nation:

A large aggregate of people united by a common descent, history, culture or language, inhabiting a particular country or territory.

ResoNation:

A combination of these two terms signifying a nation of people who are united and ready to be heard, and the amplification of their collective national voice.

A SOFT REVOLUTION FOR A 21ST CENTURY AMERICA

"Government is instituted for the common good...the people alone have an incontestable, unalienable, and indefeasible right to institute government; and to reform, alter, or totally change the same, when their protection, safety, prosperity, and happiness require it."
John Adams

****

"One of the best ways to get yourself a reputation as a dangerous citizen these days is to go about repeating the very phrases which our Founding Fathers used in the great struggle for independence."
Charles Beard

****

"First they ignore you, then they laugh at you, then they fight you, then you win."
Mohandas K. Gandhi "Mahatma"

THE END

It may seem odd to start with "The End" at the beginning of a book but, in the interest of saving your valuable time, and knowing that people have a tendency to browse the first few pages of a book before diving in, I offer the following:

THE PLAN

ResoNation describes a means to ensure that our elected officials – from the town dog catcher to the members of Congress and the President him or herself – are beholden to us, "We-the-People," rather than to "Big Money" and a selfish sub-class of special interest groups. How will we accomplish this?

ELIMINATING THE MIDDLEMAN

As described in greater detail in the following chapters, **we will transfer decision-making power from our often conflicted and corrupted elected officials to "We-the-People" via an ingenious series of local, state, regional and national "town halls" where we will decide important issues via a similarly ascending order of direct referendums.**

Note: throughout this book, when referring to voting, the terms "referendum," "direct democracy," and "initiative" are used interchangeably.

In essence this will be the most direct form of democracy in the world. Instead of voting for *people* who may or may not keep their promises and remain honest, we will vote directly to decide the *issues* that we have heretofore entrusted to them.

A wonderful cadre of intelligent and caring people from literally every demographic background – rich, poor, Jew, Christian, Muslim, Bahai, Hindu, Buddhist, atheist, agnostic, Democrat, Republican, Libertarian, Green, gay, straight, Liberal, Conservative and "None of the above," – contributed to what you are about to read. So if, you'll keep an open mind and make it through to the back cover of this purposely provocative book, you will be well on the way to counting yourself among the "founding fathers and mothers of 21st Century America."

Together, we will use *ResoNation* as an initial developmental platform for an amazing Website **(www.daylightforum.org)** where our goal will be to raise whatever dollar amount it takes to transform our current form of government into one that is highly responsive to We-the-People; one that will restore our international reputation; make our world a better, safer, place; and markedly improve our economy and standard of living. This "financial horsepower" will also ensure that the DayLight Forum will not be "just another voice among the multitudes crying out for justice."

Before you dismiss such an ambitious goal as unattainable, please permit me to remind you of Howard Dean, a little known Governor from the state of Vermont. In the 2000 presidential primary Dean shocked the political establishment by raising $50 million, at an average contribution from grassroots donors of $80 each; all on the strength of an idea that he could pull America back from its current suicidal course to one that would restore our peace and safety and raise our standard of living.

Unfortunately Governor Dean's plan had a fatal flaw. It relied on the support of one of the very entities that has gotten us into so much trouble: the Democratic Party. Don't get me wrong. He could have been running on the Republican ticket and the result would likely have been the same. Neither party can deliver what we really need: an unbiased, nonpartisan, means of ensuring that our true needs are fulfilled virtually in real time rather than every four years (if then).

Most of the money that we raise will go to three crucial civic functions:

1) Identifying a new breed of "Ombudsman-Congressmen and women" described in the chapters that follow;

2) Making the DayLight Forum *the* platform for pushing the local, state, regional and national referendum system described herein; and,

3) With or without that referendum system, dragging our political decision making process into the bright light of day.

We will accomplish this via a series of initiatives, one of which will be to support the kind of truly investigative bloggers who will become a new "Check" in our nation's Checks & Balances system. You, by the way, can and should be one of them.

Don't worry; we will still have a Congress and political parties. The difference will be that we will identify, back financially, and vote for the best person or solution rather than along rigid party lines. They can be Republican, Democrat, Green, Libertarian, gay, straight, Christian, Muslim, Jew, atheist, or any other religious, racial, political or cultural persuasion. The only requirement being that they are the best for the job. Think of it as the ultimate in **"political thinking outside the box."**

To help ensure mission success, we have engaged the Web Strategist who designed the Dean presidential Website that revolutionized American politics and raised that previously mentioned $50 million to fund a soft revolution that was intended to provide us with a better form of government and a better life for all. Armed with the lessons learned by the Dean campaign, we can bring something even greater – something that embraces *all* political parties – to life.

If Howard Dean could raise $50 million on the Democratic side and George Bush raised twice that amount on the Republican side, think of what good people from *both* sides – people who are sick and tired of being sick and tired of the same old government bureaucracy – can do now that we have a viable alternative like the one, of which you are about to read.

FOREWORD

When I was growing up, columnist and Pulitzer Prize winner, Art Buchwald, was one of my literary heroes. I'd like to borrow a line from Art that sums up my feelings about the Bush Administration and both sides of the aisle in Congress: "I'm not a Democrat or a Republican. I'm against whoever is in power." This book is about changing that increasingly popular mindset to one where our elected officials are treasured for their wisdom and guidance and our world becomes a better and safer place.

As I'm sure was the case with many of you, the events of 9/11 caused me to think beyond myself and my immediate needs and to consider what was happening to humanity, our earth and where we, as a nation, are headed. The more I studied, inquired, and thought, I realized that the solutions we need to ensure a better, safer, world were not going to come from our existing, anachronistic, political parties and form of government and that the time to replace them with something better, something more responsive to mankind's needs, is growing short.

So, four years ago, I started researching and writing *ResoNation*. Lately, I have been encouraged by the fact that many of the things that I proposed during that period, for which I was often castigated, are now widely accepted. The public's view of both political parties as feckless entities, and our invasion of Iraq are just two examples. A more recent one is an editorial in the March 14, 2006 edition of *The New York Times* ("Drop Out of the College") calling for an end to our Electoral College method of selecting a president and referring to it as an "antidemocratic relic." The editorial opined that, "It focuses presidential elections on just a handful of battleground states, and pushes the rest of the nation's voters to the sidelines" and went on to say, "[It] discriminates among voters by weighing presidential votes unequally. A Wyoming voter has about four times as much impact on selecting that state's electors as a California voter does on selecting that state's ... Sidestepping the Electoral College would be in [the] worthy tradition of making American democracy more democratic."

Trying to drink out of a fire hydrant: I honestly began to wonder whether this book would ever get published, not for lack of a publisher but because, every day, television, radio, print and Internet news sources present an overwhelming flow of new candidates for inclusion. Most deserve our earnest consideration in a public forum like the one proposed here. My greatest challenge was trying to decide which should be emphasized and in what order. As the chapters unfolded, it became clear that the answer was not "which topic to choose first" but rather **"what single act can catalyze a rational process to effectively address all of them?"** I believe the answer lies within **The DayLight Movement**, which you will read about in the pages that follow.

As America awakens to the reality of a bi-partisan failure of leadership, at both the state and federal levels, that has wreaked havoc on literally every aspect of our economy and society, the solutions offered by *ResoNation* cannot come soon enough.

HOW TO READ THIS BOOK

First and foremost, read *ResoNation* with an open mind. It is intended to become your book as much, if not more than, mine. In fact, if it were not for the conventional requirements of publishing, and securing my reader's trust, I would not even identify myself as the author because the social movement described herein did not come from me; it came from countless conversations with fellow Americans of every race, creed, nationality and income level about how we all can make our country and the world a better, safer, place.

At times, we are going to speak the unspoken – things that our "politically correct society" has made us fearful to express. Some of the statements and viewpoints offered herein may or may not hold up under vigorous debate. None are intended to be insulting or harsh. All are primarily intended to stimulate a national conversation, with you as an important participant – a conversation that starts here and will carry on at the **DayLight Forum** Website (www.daylightforum.com) as it is described in the following chapters. To me, it does not matter which side you take on any particular subject – there is certainly more than one side to many of the issues covered here. If you are provoked to join the discussion I will have done my job. So, if you like what you read, step up and lend a hand. If you don't like what you read, then speak up and help set the record straight.

The degree of relevance and weight that any individual's comments carry will be determined by the aggregated preponderance of similar expressions by all who respond. You will find a number of nifty pieces of technology at the DayLight Forum Website. One is an elegantly simple means to have effective dialogue amongst literally millions of us, simultaneously, without anarchy and with a level of civility and clarity that will permit us to register what's really important to each of us. The other will permit us to register our responses, forming a virtual "heat map" of our nation's desires, goals and the best means to achieve them. Then, as described in the following chapters, we will put them to a vote in a manner that truly represents our wishes, not those of Big Money or too-narrowly focused special interest groups.

The transformative governmental concept described herein is what our forefathers, and even many recent national leaders, intended our democracy to be. You will "hear" their voices clearly calling for it in the quotes that are respectfully interspersed throughout this book. Thus, what I am proposing is nothing really new. What is new is that the time to affect this "soft revolution" has never been better or more urgent. It is important to note that the beauty of what is being proposed here is that, even if it is not fully adopted, a tremendous amount of good can come just from the debate of this and many other issues that will take place at the DayLight Forum.

George W. Bush and the Bush Administration are mentioned frequently throughout this book because their actions demand it and because they are the ones currently in power. Despite the fact that he will be out of office in two years, *ResoNation* will remain timely as long as our current, perpetually dysfunctional, political environment continues to exist.

Occasionally you will notice a repetition of certain concepts and facts among some chapters. This is because many of the challenges that affect us, and our world, overlap and flow into a recurrent theme: i.e., that our current form of government is outmoded, inefficient, ineffective, and, if not corrupt, at least conflicted. I have tried to keep this repetition to a minimum so that you can get through *ResoNation* and start taking action as soon as possible.

Time and space simply would not permit every subject that rightfully deserves exploration to be covered here but I promise that we will dutifully address all that you care about at the DayLight Forum. Likewise, some chapters are markedly shorter than others for the simple reason that ResoNation is not intended to be an exhaustive treatise on every subject (e.g. mandatory sentencing; hypocritical marijuana laws while millions of us die from alcohol; global warming and the environment; etc.) but rather a *starting point* for a list of things that are being frequently discussed across America and throughout the world – a debate that can only reach consensus when each topic is decided by a truly democratic vote. Let us begin.

INTRODUCTION

A 21st Century System for A 21st Century Democracy

This is the story of a nation that spent two hundred years searching for a true and truthful leader and ultimately found 300 million of them. In course of their discovery process they found a way to elevate their government from an impermanent, oft-changing system of leadership to a permanent and reliable one that responds directly to the collective intelligence of We-the-People.

> **"Many forms of Government have been tried, and will be tried in this world of sin and woe. No one pretends that democracy is perfect or all-wise. Indeed it has been said that democracy is the worst form of Government except all those other forms that have been tried from time to time."** *Sir Winston Churchill*

While the structure of democracy has not changed significantly in the past three hundred years, its values and environment have. In the last century, the radio, telephone, television, and the Internet have all become commonplace to most of America. Combined into a synergistic whole, these technological advances present an opportunity to bring our current form of democracy into the 21st century for the betterment of all. Just as large corporations would no more persist in using outmoded mimeographs, telegraphs, and paper-and-penciled accounting sheets to match the speed and agility of their competitors, why should We-the-People live and operate under an equally slow-to-react system of government? Speed, flexibility, and the ability to acquire and employ information are requisite to the maintenance of our status as a world leader: a status that is diminishing under a load of national debt and corrupt leadership decisions, and in the face of competition for markets and resources from a burgeoning European Union and a rising China.

Our current form of government-by-representation was created largely out of geographical convenience and a belief that, lacking a national education system, most American citizens were too ignorant to know what was best for them. Timing, distance, and a growing population's sheer numbers made it difficult, if not logistically impossible, for all to convene in one place every time a matter of regional or national importance had to be decided. So our founding fathers created a system by which we would choose the most educated among us to represent our best interests and work and reside in our nation's capitol or in their respective state capitols.

That once-effective system worked well for a time but, like any organization, it eventually fell prey to bureaucracy, growth for growth's sake, and a conflict-of-interest derived from the fact that it became so prohibitively expensive to become elected and to remain in office that our representatives can no longer realistically represent us because they are beholden to whomever writes the checks that keep them in power. Thus, our government has grown into a labyrinthine, bureaucratic "rat's nest" of convoluted processes, make-work, and influence peddling – or as the humorist Will Rogers put it, "the best government money can buy." Echoing that sentiment in the more recent past, in a July 7, 1999 piece David Broder of *The Washington Post* reported that, "Senator John McCain (R-Ariz.) opines that American politics has become 'an influence-peddling scheme in which both parties compete to stay in office by selling the country to the highest bidder.'" By kowtowing to a president whose campaign slandered him in the 2000 presidential primary, it appears that the good senator himself is not above selling out.

When you have someone else fight your battles, you give up a significant degree of control over your life and your destiny and, when the "chosen ones" fail to admit that they no longer represent you, how can you possibly win? The 21st century offers us both the technology to level the playing field and, thanks to our national education system, a population (according to a perhaps overly optimistic U.S. Census Bureau) bearing a 97% literacy rate, that is capable of learning about and addressing the issues and challenges that confront us. Thus, we now have a viable alternative:

Government by Local, State, Regional and National Referendum: There has never been a more appropriate time in our nation's history to move our current form of governmental decision-making toward a system of direct decision making by We-the-People. We will start in the polling booth and, with the same ingenuity and can-do spirit that put a man on moon, we will migrate our decision-making process out of the Big Money, special-interest-lobbying cesspool of our current Congress and into the bright light of day.

When we know that a serious mistake has been made, such as the failure to properly anticipate and prepare for local resistance in Iraq, why do we have to wait as many as four years for a change of administration to cure the problem and stop the needless loss of American and foreign lives? A national referendum sure beats taking polls while our young men and women are dying on foreign soil. Unlike contests that just elect *people*, these issue-oriented contests will forego the mudslinging personal attacks that poison our current political process. In addition, direct referendum voting will eliminate bill-swapping, which demeans the voting process on a number of levels and further removes control from We-the-People. Such under-the-table deals, made in some office in Washington, do not represent the sentiment or the values of We-the-People. What Thomas Jefferson hoped would never come to pass has become the norm, and it is time we seriously reconsider his words:

> **"States can best govern our home concerns and the general government our foreign ones. I wish, therefore... never to see all offices transferred to Washington, where, further withdrawn from the eyes of the people, they may more secretly be bought and sold at market."**

While our President, his Cabinet, and many government administrative offices can remain where they are, our true nation's capitol will no longer need to be in Washington, D.C. It will be on your telephone keypad, under a postage stamp, and eventually on your computer desktop – and, if you wish, you will still be able to go to a conventional polling place.

Plato reminds us that, *"[t]he penalty good men pay for indifference to public affairs is to be ruled by evil men;"* and so it goes that even the most brilliant and bulletproof referendum system will not work on the strength of a concept or because technology makes it possible. This kind of change will necessitate the active backing of a massive number of citizens with a passion for the fairest and most representative form of government attainable; one that empowers the individual voter and limits influence peddlers and their targets by dragging them into the light of day. This kind of passion requires a catalyst – i.e. a *forum and a platform* of beliefs that can embrace the widest possible audience.

As proposed in the pages that follow, this robust, information-rich platform will be built on things that truly resonate among all of us. Those who look at issues solely from a self-centered perspective may attack some platform positions as "wrong" or "politically incorrect;" but We-the-People are going to have to unlearn our self-centered national behavior so that, instead of focusing on what we have to lose, we will focus on what we have to gain as individuals and as a nation. President John F. Kennedy's call to, *"Ask not what your country can do for you, ask what you can do for your country"* has never been more important or more relevant.

THE DAYLIGHT MOVEMENT

ResoNation is the first plank of a comprehensive tri-part platform, called **The DayLight Movement**, which includes an information-rich multimedia Internet forum, the **DayLight Forum (www.daylightforum.org)**, and in the not-too-distant future, an Internet (and, perhaps eventually, a traditional) radio talk show called **DayLight Radio** that will be manned by DayLight volunteers. The movement as a whole is meant to be a commonsense people's movement; one that can provide the clearest and most direct way for a nation to truly speak its mind, set its course, and achieve its greatest destiny.

Hopi Indian elders have a saying, "We are the One's we've been waiting for." Like our Founding Fathers did when they created our Constitution, the charter drafters of this movement will likely be drawn from the people who read this book and then decide to do something about the challenges described between its covers.

> **"A man who thinks of himself as belonging to a particular national group in America has not yet become an American."**
> *Woodrow Wilson*

It is important that We-the-People remember that we are neither liberals nor conservatives; we are first and foremost *Americans*, a concept that has been all but lost in the current environment of partisan politics. *ResoNation* is about transforming our current form of government into one that represents We-the-People, rather than one that panders to those who can pay the most to have themselves heard. It describes a means for Americans to radically-but-not-anarchically restructure our local and national government into a system that puts Big Money, the military-industrial complex, special interest groups, their lobbyists, liberal and conservative politicians, and the American people all on the same side of literally every issue. It all starts with a single question: "What's good for America?"

> **"For too long we've been told about 'us' and 'them.' Each and every election we see a new slate of arguments and ads telling us**

that 'they' are the problem, not 'us.' But there can be no 'them' in America. There's only us." *William Jefferson Clinton*

For starters, We-the-People need to stop kidding ourselves that we elect our leaders. One needs to look no further than the 2000 and 2004 presidential elections. Corruption, Big Money, special interests, character assassination, and flat-out lies get people elected; and we aid and abet this travesty by becoming so jaded and discouraged that even proof of lies and wrongdoing are not enough to make us speak out. Why? Because we have learned that "it won't do any good" and that we are powerless in the face of a bureaucracy and political machine system that has grown more powerful than those who it is supposed to serve.

To paraphrase Mark Twain:

Everyone complains about the never-ending stream of trouble with our current form of government, but no one does anything about it.

This book offers a means to do something proactive and constructive, and to have the voice of the people truly resonate in the ears of politicians who have ignored us for too long.

When something is truly right, we feel it in our gut; it calls up and cross-references with all the things we have learned. One could say that it *resonates* within us and emboldens us to trust our judgments about life and the world around us. When such a truth is *shared*, it resonates amongst *all of us* as if a giant bell had been struck. Isn't this the message that our forefathers intended with the iconic image of the Liberty Bell? It is time, once again, to strike a chord with the American people and let truth and freedom ring throughout our great nation.

The once-noble practice of politics and governance has become more about concentrated power than about the people's needs. *ResoNation's* primary purpose is to stimulate a national discussion of the things that politicians steer clear of, tethered as they are to their Big Money, special interest masters and to "political correctness."

ResoNation does not end at its back cover. It is meant to be a portal to that previously mentioned rich interactive environment called the DayLightForum.org a public meeting place on the Web that will act as a local, state, regional, and national town hall where each of us, regardless of race, creed, political affiliation, education level or financial standing, can tangibly contribute to improving America and the world at large – and do it in broad daylight.

A charter group of DayLight volunteers, will moderate this highly interactive public forum. The dialogue that starts here will continue over the airwaves, in the press, in town halls and places of worship, and, most importantly, in our homes. We do not necessarily have to agree with the opinions and insights stated in the DayLight venues described herein but we owe it to ourselves and to our nation to openly and honestly discuss them, and to respect all who care enough to participate.

> **"It should be the highest ambition of every American to extend his views beyond himself, and to bear in mind that his conduct will not only affect himself, his country, and his immediate posterity; but that its influence may be co-extensive with the world, and stamp political happiness or misery on ages yet unborn."**
> *George Washington*

At no time in the history of journalism and mass media has there been a greater opportunity to, as George Washington advised, be seen and heard in an effective manner that can ignite the public's interest and actually engage their participation in worthy causes. Internet Websites, like the DayLight Forum, that are tailored to specific audiences who can readily find and subscribe to them via a technology called **RSS** (Really Simple Syndication); conventional radio; Internet radio; subscription satellite radio; and podcasts that can be downloaded and played at any time, ensure that anyone with a worthwhile message can be seen and heard.

The latest addition to the world of journalism and media combines the best attributes of all of these media into a cost-effective medium called **Slivercasting**. One of the challenges of producing a successful television program has been the need to find a large enough audience to make production economically feasible. The ease of digital video production and the ubiquity of high-speed Internet connections permit creation of specialized video offerings that would normally appeal to only a small "sliver" of a conventional television audience. That audience can now be easily aggregated on the Internet and grow "virally" through word-of-mouth, Internet linking, and the above-mentioned RSS subscription tool.

The third plank of the DayLight Movement, **DayLight Radio**, will speak to an audience that falls into the great divide between the Sean Hannitys and Rush Limbaughs on one side, and the Randi Rhodes and Al Frankens on the other: an audience that is tired of conservative vs. liberal programs that constantly attack the other side rather than finding actual solutions to the challenges that face all of us as. Don't get me wrong; these radio hosts are, for the most part, my heroes. They provide a valuable service that will be even more so when we all have a defined place to effect real change rather than just talk about it. As it is used throughout this book, the term "DayLight Radio," applies to traditional broadcast radio, podcasting and two-way Internet radio – technologies that are available virtually anywhere in the civilized world, 24 hours a day.

A common characteristic of the various facets of the DayLight Forum and DayLight Radio is that they will constitute a literal, nonpartisan, *community of conversations* about how to make America safe and great once again. We have learned that conversations that simply bat around the liberal or conservative agendas do not solve anything; we need to start actually talking to each other about the *American* agenda.

While I was writing this book, an acquaintance posed the following question: *"What is America and what is an American? How do all 300 million of us arrive at the same answer when asked: What's good for America? Do I have the same priorities as a Hawaiian, or an Alaskan, or a New Yorker?"*

The answer, of course, is that we do indeed have different values. That is why *ResoNation* describes a powerful means to *push decision-making back down to the grassroots level*, thereby putting control back in the hands of the people who are actually affected by decisions that concern them on a daily basis. The centerpiece of this DayLight concept of governance is the DayLight Forum where important issues can be addressed in the bright light of day and where We-the-People and not some gang of pandering politicians, will *learn, consider,* and *decide* what is right for us. I'm not talking about doing away with our current political parties. I'm simply advocating a logical evolution of their quality and wisdom.

To those who say that our current elected leaders will never permit this evolution – this ethics transformation – to happen, I ask, "What politician is going to come out against open-book, virtually corruption and conflict-of-interest-free, government? Especially if they can still remain in office simply by supporting our national initiative and if they can be supported by a fund that we, not Big Money or selfish special interests will raise and spend in support of the best of them.

> **"Native Americans have a saying: 'No tree has branches so foolish as to fight among themselves.'"** *Dr. Wayne Dyer*

Like you, I am an American who is tired of backbiting among all of the factions that have increasingly divided our nation, and that have made the concept of a collective people's voice all but impossible. Whites vs. minorities, liberals vs. conservatives, Republicans vs. Democrats vs. Greens vs. Libertarians, rich vs. poor – we are a nation divided when we do not have to be. Within the new DayLight system, we can still call ourselves "conservatives" or "liberals" or anything else that we want; but, first and foremost, we are all *Americans* who need to band together in an increasingly hostile world.

We-the-People are dying on foreign battlefields and in our own country for causes and reasons that don't resonate with the ring of truth. We didn't have the money to fund the agents that the FBI and CIA needed to monitor and head-off the al Qaeda's of the world, but we found $900 Billion to invade a country that turns out to have been a relative "paper tiger" and another $100 Billion to chase Osama bin Laden and his crew in Afghanistan. Far too many of our fellow Americans are dying of hunger while we spend billions to curry favor with fanatic countries that may fear us but will never respect us. Meanwhile, our roads and bridges crumble, we are dying from diseases caused by the damage that those who we trusted to represent us have foisted onto our environment, and our education system permits our children to lag far behind nations that we are supposedly superior to.

As a nation we are rotting from within after years of apathy and resignation about what we, as individuals, can do to reset our national course. The "DayLight Movement," and its "DayLight Forum" provide a source of solutions that all of us can buy into because we will create them.

NO "CHECKS & BALANCES" JUST CHECKS FROM BIG MONEY AND SPECIAL INTEREST GROUPS

Before we proceed, it will be helpful to differentiate between two frequently used terms: "Big Money" and "Big Business." Big Business is a good thing; it means that someone has worked diligently to develop, market, and sell a product or a service that people need. A positive by-product of the good that Big Business generates, "Big Money," can also be a corrupting influence.

> **"If Congress can do whatever in their discretion can be done by money, and will promote the General Welfare, then the Government is no longer a limited one, possessing enumerated powers, but an indefinite one, subject to particular exceptions."**
> *James Madison*

We no longer have Checks and Balances; we have checks from Big Money and special interest groups. We are fooling ourselves if we think that we live in a true democracy. What we have is an *oligarchy of special interest groups*, the goals of which are not those of the people but rather of a select cohort of corporations and wealthy individuals. In his stellar primer on the power and the future of the Internet in politics titled, *The Revolution Will Not Be Televised*, former Dean campaign manager, Internet and political strategy master, Joe Trippi, commented on the $125 million raised by George W. Bush for his second presidential campaign: "In effect, sixty thousand rich white guys [at roughly $2,000 each] determined who would be president for the rest of us three hundred million people. And this is not an aberration. Each year, the richest one quarter of 1 percent of Americans make 80 percent of all political donations."

This is not to say that there is anything wrong with being wealthy; it is, after all, built into the larger concept of the American Dream. But being wealthy ceases to be a virtue when it comes at the expense of others, and this has become a disturbingly common practice in today's world.

There are groups, such as the unions and AARP, that represent the interests of vast segments of our population very admirably; but these groups represent *Americans* and not some amorphous, often faceless, corporate interest, concept or agenda fronted by professional lobbyists with access to people and information that we could never hope to obtain. The groups that are the most troubling are those with narrow special interests that, in some cases, have little to do with what is good for America and more to do with what is good for a particular industry, religious or social group, or even another country. When, to the detriment of the general population, a special interest group stops considering the greater good in favor of its own narrow agenda, it becomes necessary to speak out. That time is now. We-the-People must take our country back.

"From time to time, we have been tempted to believe that society has become too complex to be managed by self-rule, that government by an elite group is superior to government for, by, and of the people. But if no one among us is capable of governing himself, then who among us has the capacity to govern someone else? All of us together, in and out of government, must bear the burden."
Ronald Reagan, 1981 Inaugural

I believe that, if Ronald Reagan, "the Great Communicator," were alive today, in this Internet age, he would be advocating something very similar to the DayLight Movement and its drive to clean up and simplify government.

The only thing that can save us from drowning in our current bureaucratic mess is for We-the-People to pull together, but this cannot be just another nifty phrase to mouth. We must decide to truly work and learn. An educated electorate – one that knows how to question authority and is willing to do so – is far less likely to become dominated by any particular interest group. Let us pull together for an informed America where there is only one special interest group and one lobbying target: the American people.

"I think we all have a need to know what we do not need to know."
William Safire

LOBBYING IN BROAD DAYLIGHT

"Push to Tighten Lobbying Rules Loses Strength" The New York Times March 10, 2006:

"The drive for a tighter lobbying law, just two months ago a major priority on Capitol Hill, is losing momentum, a victim of shifting political interests, infighting among House Republicans and a growing sense among lawmakers of both parties that wholesale change may not be needed after all… Further, Congress tends to have a short attention span. Without a grass-roots hue and cry of the sort that pushed lawmakers to block the Dubai port deal in March of 2006, it was perhaps inevitable that the push for lobbying law changes would diminish."

It is important to remember that, as corrupt as it has become of late, lobbying is a powerful force that is firmly embedded in our national fabric. Reso-Nation offers a new system of government, one in which lobbyists will still lobby and spend billions of their clients' dollars doing so, and special interest groups will still press their agendas and spend billions more doing so. The only difference will be that these individuals will have to direct all of their persuasive tactics to We-the-People, rather than to politicians who, in order to remain in power, are forced to seek favor from self-interested financial masters instead of from the people who they are sworn to represent.

The beauty of this form of governance is that it brings a healthy dose of reality to related subjects like "honor in Congress" and "lobbying." For example, under the DayLight system, lobbyists can, within reason, do virtually anything they want and Congressmen and women can accept virtually any favor because those transactions, and our entire government, will all be conducted in the bright light of day. Lobbying that is forced into the open is far less likely to be dangerous to our individual and national wellbeing. You cannot legislate human greed and frailty away but you can drag it into daylight.

When my children were growing up, I borrowed a phrase, "Roof top shout" from a book, entitled *"Helping Your Child Learn Right from Wrong, Values Clarification,"* by Dr. Sidney B. Simon and Sally Wendkos Olds, which offers a simple seven-step process for reacting to any situation or temptation. The idea behind "Roof top shout" is, "Before you do something, would you be willing to climb up onto your roof and shout your intention to the world? If not then don't do it." We can help our elected leaders put that simple "truth tool" into practice by putting them on the rooftop of the DayLight Forum.

TAKING ACTION

The DayLight Movement is about Americans who are terrified about our financial future, our children's future, and our national safety. No single leader or political administration can save America from threats to these basic aspects of a happy life. Only We-the-People can save our nation from the forces of greed, evil, and plain bumbling that operate within our current systems of government and commerce.

"Knowing is not enough; we must apply. Understanding is not enough; we must do. Knowing and understanding in action make for honor. And honor is the heart of wisdom." - *Johann von Goethe*

To be fair, the fact that our political leaders have not and cannot save us is not entirely their fault. Our present system of governance and leadership is simply not up to the challenges of modern-day America. If it were, millions of Americans would not be going to bed hungry every night; we would not be mired in literally trillions of dollars worth of debt; we would not be engaged in wars that do not need to be fought; and we would not be playing benefactor to countries whose citizens hate or, at best, disdain us for our government's imperialistic, bullying ways. Solving unemployment, saving our environment, combating terrorism, improving our education system – all are important, but these are just symptoms of a greater challenge that must be faced, and solved, by We-the-People. What is most important is that we **bring our system of government into the 21st century.**

Our current democratic system was created before the telephone, radio, television, and the Internet were invented. Because today's technology enables something far better, it is both the right time and our duty to become agents of change.

Radio talk-show host Randi Rhodes has said that, *"there is no conscience in American politics any more."* Well, I believe that we do indeed have a conscience, but it has been suppressed by fear and lies perpetrated by our elected leaders. For the first time in history, the technology to get to the truth is available to the average American. All we need is a reliable means and place to access it. The DayLight Forum is that place; a place where we can aggregate our greater collective consciousness into a veritable "Master Mind" via **a truly democratic, virtually real-time, voting process** as described in the following pages. When this new, interactive, governmental operating system is in place we will be able to decide how best to tackle the massive challenges that loom larger each day.

PART ONE:
THE MOVEMENT

CHAPTER 1

THE DAYLIGHT MOVEMENT

KNOWLEDGE IS POWER

> **"People who expect to be ignorant and free expect what never was and never will be."** *Thomas Jefferson*

The DayLight Movement is based on a belief that it is information and education, not money and military might, that will make our nation and its people strong. In the DayLight Movement, We-the-People will have an Internet-based, real-time information resource and our own media network for all to use for learning, for decision-making, and for assurance that the news we receive remains fair and balanced – a term that has been greatly demeaned by certain news sources upon which we have had to rely for much of our knowledge of current affairs.

When the American people are honestly and truthfully informed and the time comes that the lobbyists and special interest groups have to direct their pitches to We-the-People, all of their marketing and persuasion tactics will have to be honest and factual or we will see through their deceit. By the same token, the press will become more investigative and less biased and sensationalistic because We-the-People will be wise to them as well.

A fairly recent, Internet-based, international "Neighborhood Watch," which we will explore in later pages, is a phenomenon called "blogging:" online diaries and running commentaries on a wide array of topics by ordinary citizens as well as the "high & mighty" of government and commerce. Bloggers help to keep traditional news sources and virtually everyone else honest. I have witnessed when someone tried to "pull a fast one," in the conventional press or in the "blogosphere" and several hundred citizen bloggers jumped all over the offending statement, dragging it into the bright light of day.

The cover story of the May 2, 2005 edition of *Business Week*, titled, *"Blogs Will Change Your Business,"* asserts that *"[t]he divide between the publishers and the public is collapsing. This turns mass media upside down. It creates media of the masses."* The article, written by Stephen Baker and

Heather Green, went on to report that it is already possible for an organization to track millions of blogs simultaneously. The result is "a heat map of what... the world is thinking about, minute by minute." The DayLight Forum will effectively extend "blog power" to all who visit it and participate in its myriad discussions.

With all of this technology at our fingertips, it is fair to say that We-the-People have the potential to become the most enlightened and responsible voting population in the history of the world. Using the DayLight Forum as our staging area, we will have *the power to effect change, virtually in real-time*, without having to wait for "Big Brother" to schedule a vote, because we can initiate the process on our own. Votes on important issues will resonate with a ring of fairness and truth. Even when a vote goes against a particular position that you or I support, we will know that it was fair, for the greater good, and not for the benefit of some special interest minority, lurking in a proverbial "back room" with a bag full of cash and favors. With telephone and cell phone, conventional voting machines, and eventually with our computers via the Internet, we can be more proactive and able to send a virtually instant message whenever our country and its leaders get off of a track that We-the-People, not they, will lay. For the first time in modern history the average American citizen, who currently feels overwhelmed and helpless to change anything, will be empowered to "move the proverbial ball."

Our country's soul is slipping away so quickly that the time for action is *now*. We are living in an ever-more competitive world, where the greatness or downfall of a nation is determined by the intelligence and dedicated interest of its citizens. This does not necessarily mean that one must have attended college, but we do need to be well informed to effect change in an ever-shrinking, increasingly turbulent, world. The DayLight Movement provides an impartial information resource and a virtual series of local, state, regional and national town halls expressly for that purpose. It is more important than ever that all of us become informed voters, because if we are not educated and do not vote, then we will have no one to blame but ourselves for the things that happen to us, to our loved ones, and to our nation.

> **"One oft-stated goal of democracy is the growth of individuals. Hence, the double meaning of "self-government;" in the course of participating in public affairs, individuals become more complete people (or "selves") with richer lives. The converse is equally true:**

if self-government promotes better, more mature selves, so too the latter makes effective self-government possible. Unless citizens develop sufficient knowledge, independence, and public spiritedness, they cannot handle the responsibilities of self-government."
Alan Hirsch

As we struggle to keep up with an increasingly fast-paced world, our national resonance, which used to be based on commonsense, has faded to a whisper. Through our electoral process, we have surrendered responsibility for our well-being to those who claim to be more knowledgeable and better equipped to address important matters of state like our nation's economy, education, defense, health care, transportation, market regulation, and justice, to name just a few. What good is our vote if we entrust it to people who do not serve our interests?

"There is this strange disease that affects Republicans as well as Democrats, that as soon as you get away from home, you think your ideas are better than at the grassroots."
Senator Lamar Alexander, R. Tennessee

IT'S NOT JUST THE LOBBYISTS

Our precious votes have fallen prey to a bizarre cross-weave of conflicting electoral challenges and proposals. A prime example of this is a 2004 ballot measure (which failed to pass) to change Colorado's state constitution so that its nine electoral votes would be allocated in proportion to the popular vote, instead of on a winner-take-all basis. While this move would keep the electoral vote in line with the way citizens actually voted it also supports the logic behind simply doing away with the Electoral College altogether. Doing so would dramatically reduce the inordinate amount of power held by some of America's special interest groups whose members tend to concentrate in states with large metropolitan areas and heavy electoral voting power.

How do you feel about the fact that the winner of the 2000 presidential election received fewer votes than the loser? Would you be surprised to learn that this was not the first time? It happened in 1824, 1876 and as recently as 1960. Whether you voted for Al Gore in 2000 or not, it makes a person wonder whether we'd be bogged down in Iraq – a 21st century "Viet Nam" – if politicians not so beholden to the military-industrial-complex were in power.

By becoming passive spectators on our local and national political playing fields we have unintentionally fostered a sickening degree of hubris and a twisted sense of entitlement that resonates, to our detriment, through the halls of Congress and America's corporate boardrooms. As a nation, we are rapidly losing sight of our values. It is time that We-the-People take definitive action to change our electoral system from one of corruptible power to one of wisdom and honest guidance. In the March 14, 2006 editorial mentioned in this book's Forward, ("Drop Out of the College"), *The New York Times* opined, "... throughout the nation's history, there have been a series of reforms affecting how elections are conducted, like the ones that gave blacks and women the vote and provided for the direct election of United States senators." If we can directly elect our Congressmen and women, then why not the leader of the free world?

What do you say about a country and an electorate that, during the Democratic Party's 2004 presidential primaries, selected its nominee not because of what he stood for but because they felt he could defeat the incumbent Republican – a man who many claim bought his 2000 and 2004 elections? What do you say about an electorate that was so cowed by the "propaganda of fear" that it elected a president who is neither popular nor wise, and is either an outright liar or a dupe of his political handlers? What do you say about the leverage held by special interest groups and Big Money corporations, and the mindset of voters that elect as senator a woman who, as honorable and wise as she may be, did not live in the state that elected her prior to running for office? This is not representation; this is pure old power and manipulation. We-the-People deserve better.

"What good fortune for governments that people do not think."
Adolph Hitler

"Thinking" must start with conversations. Coffee house conversations are great but something better defined and organized is needed. Something that can sustain millions of simultaneous conversations and organize them in such a way that patterns can be readily detected, and fair and rational conclusions can be drawn and acted upon by the people themselves. The DayLight Forum has such a tool and will be perfecting its capability over time.

AN AMERICAN CONVERSATION

Young people especially need to secure their future by supporting The DayLight Movement rather than the PR-driven partisan cliques that our political parties have become. We need to talk less about what our country needs to do and start talking about what we, as *individuals*, need to do. The DayLight system is not a panacea; we all know that there is no such thing as a perfect system for any purpose. Instead, it represents a good starting point for one of the most important and exciting conversations in the history of our nation – one that requires the active participation of *all* Americans in a free-flowing interaction that will lead us to where we, as a nation, want to be.

> **"I know no safe depository of the ultimate powers of the society but the people themselves; and if we think them not enlightened enough to exercise their control with a wholesome discretion, the remedy is not to take it from them, but to inform their discretion by education."** *Thomas Jefferson*

THE MYTH OF COMPLEXITY AND FEAR OF THE MAJORITY

To those who say that the issues facing our country are too complex and too time-consuming for its citizens to command, it is worthwhile to repeat the time-proven adage: "the bigger the problem, the simpler the solution." Much of that so-called "complexity" is nothing more than self-serving job creation, perpetuation, and obfuscation on the part of those whose jobs, elections, power, and riches rely on such a myth. Under the DayLight process politicians will, by definition, be honest and lobbyists will move heaven and earth to guide us to the truth or we will know it and their clients' money will be wasted.

To those who fear "decision-by-majority:" wouldn't you rather be governed by the direct expression of We-the-People rather than having our needs and aspirations filtered and edited by politicians who pander to political correctness, Big Money, and special interests? Governance by majority vote is only dangerous if the majority as well as the minority is not well informed about each particular issue or educated enough to understand it; or if the majority is dominated by illegal immigrants who have not earned the right to join in the American decision-making process. (The subject of immigration will be explored in greater depth later in this book.)

Constitutional scholar, Professor Alan, Hirsch, in his seminal treatise titled, *Direct Democracy and Civic Maturation*, argues for our right to amend our Constitution for the purpose of effecting direct voting rather than representative voting. One of the many salient points of Professor Hirsch's cogent document puts the specter of tyranny-by-majority to rest: "Does direct democracy leave minorities – including racial minorities, but also homosexuals, aliens, and other underrepresented groups – at the mercy of majorities? The risk that citizen lawmaking, will be misused to punish the weakest or least popular members of a community rests on a vision of an atomized populace voting its fears, prejudices, and unenlightened self-interests. To the extent this phenomenon exists, we should not regard it as unalterable. If the citizenry lacks civic virtue that may be because it has been alienated from civic responsibility. Involving people in the process of making laws is a step in the direction of fostering public-spiritedness. By contrast, allowing people to vote only for representatives, who often duck hard choices and place their own ambitions ahead of public service, is a prescription for a selfish and apathetic citizenry. To the extent that initiatives inspire citizens to participate in collective self government, they could prove a partial corrective."

"It does not take a majority to prevail... but rather an irate, tireless minority, keen on setting brushfires of freedom in the minds of men." *Samuel Adams*

In the 21st century, members of the minority (whomever they may be in a particular decision) have little to fear. Thanks to a ubiquitous, highly accessible media and mass communication environment (especially the Internet), anyone with a valid point can be heard. In fact, bloggers are proving that the mainstream media is now being forced to pay attention to the *most articulate*, rather than the most powerful.

"If we ever pass out as a great nation we ought to put on our tombstone, 'America died from a delusion that she has moral leadership.'" *Will Rogers*

In 1776, we embarked on the most ambitious governmental experiment in the history of the world but now we are living in a jaded America. As a nation, we have become desensitized to the fact that thousands of American soldiers have been killed and maimed in Iraq, not to mention the vast numbers of innocent Iraqi civilians (35,000 at last count) who have perished. We simply, and sadly, do not feel these things anymore – a first sign of a nation sliding into decadence and decline. Arnold Toynbee, who wrote the acclaimed 12-volume work, *A Study of History*, once declared, "Of the 22 civilizations that have appeared in history, 19 of them collapsed when they reached the moral state America is in today."

We need to awaken to the fact that we have not lost our soul; our government has lost its soul and it is time for it to upgrade to the 21st century while still retaining the values of our founding forefathers. Who else but America should lead the next paradigm-shift in the realm of human governance? When has there been a greater need or a better time?

One of the most important things to keep in mind is that, to one degree or another, anything that happens to the least of us happens to all of us. America will thrive only if we realize that we are all part of a single organism, and thus, act and vote in a manner that does not kill any one part. We have permitted ourselves to be panicked into selling out to a masterfully-orchestrated campaign of fear, which caused us to elect someone in 2004 who many of us knew in our hearts was not the best candidate for the highest office in the land. However, with the advent of print, radio, television, and the Internet (especially daily news and email services), that previously mentioned 97% literacy rate, and guidance by the "ombudsman" political prototype described below, we will be in good hands: our own.

A NEW KIND OF CONGRESSMAN

Webster's New Universal Unabridged Dictionary defines ombudsman as **"an appointed public official who investigates activities of government agencies that may infringe on the rights of individuals."**

Noble civic organizations, like Common Cause, alert We-the-People to gross political transgressions, and they work diligently to influence government policy on a case-by-case basis; but change on an order of several magnitudes greater is needed. We need a means to actually take action on the things that the "whistleblowers" call to our attention. There are some ugly issues that need to be addressed and put behind us, and they cannot be ignored any longer. Under the guidance of the DayLight Movement, politicians will be converted from their current role as decision-makers who are constantly plagued by conflicts of interest from their Big Money masters.

Instead, they will be *educators and ombudsmen* for We-the-People. We, not our elected ombudsmen, will vote on important issues via a regularly scheduled series of local, state, regional and national referendums. When necessity calls, a special panel – perhaps an elected Supreme Court, or a junior adjunct thereof in the form of a qualified (not patronage-appointed) review board, will adjudicate these referendums, which will be open and immune to undue influence.

> **Without wise leadership, a nation is in trouble; but with good counselors there is safety.** *Proverbs 11:14*

Under our voice-of-the-people form of government, we will require our elected representatives to be as informed and experienced as possible so that they can advise us about each voting issue. It is in our power to create what will be looked back upon a thousand years from now as a turning point to a world illuminated by the light of full disclosure not darkness; of peace not hatred and war; and of enlightenment, wisdom and spirituality on a level that permits us to respect, learn from, and become better *because of*, not in spite of, our differences. These qualities can be cynically characterized as "platitudes," or they can be respected as something that we all are willing to work for. The choice is ours. It all starts with a simple decision: DayLight or darkness?

> **"We can forgive a child who is afraid of the dark; the real tragedy of life is when men are afraid of the light."** *Plato*

"SOFT REVOLUTION"

Power in the hands of the federal government is not the problem; *misuse* of that power and misapplication of our money and natural resources by conflicted politicians is. We have the ability to create a new system of government that keeps the best of what we have while improving the worst into something noble, wise and effective. By adopting a national referendum system, We-the-People can lift our politicians out of their current influence-peddling cesspool and elevate them to the level of leadership, wisdom, and expertise that they all claim to possess. Once the requirement to chase Big Money is removed, we will see who really wants to serve their fellow man and who is in it just for the wealth and power. When we have cleaned up the mindset, values, and motives of our Congressmen and women, they will be free to focus on untangling our bureaucracy and transforming our government into one that actually serves its citizens with a degree of responsiveness much closer to real-time. The business world and many other countries are rapidly moving toward real-time responsiveness. Why should the government of the most powerful nation on earth remain so far behind the times?

What we are really talking about is overhauling and elevating the basic function and culture of Congress, not eliminating it. Many of the good Congressmen in office today will still be in office when the DayLight system of *people-powered governance* is fully in place. Once conflict-of-interest, the taint of Big Money, and skewed electoral influence are effectively removed from the congressional function, the leadership dynamic of our entire governmental system will dramatically improve.

"Our country has come to feel the same when Congress is in session as when a baby gets hold of a hammer." *Will Rogers*

Just one of literally thousands of reasons why We-the-People need to take actual decision making power away from Congress is the Medicare accounting scandal (reported in the March 25, 2004 edition of *The New York Times*, "Medicare Official Testifies on Cost Figures"). Medicare's actuary, Richard Foster, declared that the cost of the new Medicare bill would actually be $200 Billion *more* (an eye-popping 50% discrepancy) than what was submitted to Congress 6 months before it voted for approval. When NBC Nightly News reported that the Democrats were strongly suggesting that the issue should be re-voted, it was pointed out that *"[w]ith both houses controlled by the Republicans, there is little-to-no chance that that will happen."*

By refusing to put it to a re-vote, Congress, as the only entity able to correct this fraud, became a collaborator. If the DayLight referendum system had been active, We-the-People could have corrected this financial travesty in a matter of weeks, if not days. In fact its very existence, speed, and flexibility will affect a dynamic change in our governmental culture, emboldening government employees like Mr. Foster to be more forthcoming upon learning of such gross misdeeds.

Like most of the messes in Washington, the fault for this particular one lies with both parties. With all of their experience, money and staff, and 6 months before a vote was called, no one bothered to perform the basic due diligence that could have uncovered this egregious misrepresentation. We can do better.

We-the-People have the power to stop most if not all of the insanely illogical regulatory acts perpetrated on our pursuit of life, liberty, and happiness by the appointed minions of whatever political party happens to be in power at the time – parties that, under the current political culture, are conflicted at best and corrupt at worst. The following pages offer an initial DRAFT of a platform for The DayLight Movement. I cannot stress strongly enough that the positions and opinions recorded throughout the chapters that follow are just that – one man's opinions – offered as conversation starters to be shaped, by you, into formal platform points, but only after they have been actively argued, tested, and argued some more via the public forums that we will create and use daily. Reading this book is our first step into that future. Let us begin.

CHAPTER 2

EFFECTING NEW LEADERSHIP

PLATFORM POINTS FOR WE-THE-PEOPLE TO REBUILD AMERICA IN THE 21ST CENTURY

"Example isn't the main thing in influencing others; it's the only thing." *Albert Schweitzer*

Leaders do not have to be politicians. No one elected Albert Schweitzer, Billy Graham, C.S. Lewis, or Mother Teresa. Like cream, they naturally rose to the top by word and deed. Sadly, in today's America, "example" means little or nothing compared to the roar of money and fear mongering. We-the-People can and must change that.

The best place to start a movement for change is to define what we want from our leaders and managers. Then, as empowered voters, our job will be to ensure that the DayLight system of governance has the means to identify and select the best and brightest to educate and guide us and manage the affairs of our country. A well-thought-out selection process will ensure that the best advisor-leaders are elected and we will know if it is working because their input will be delivered to us in the bright light of day. The people who can fulfill our new criteria may very well be found among *ResoNation's* readership. They will contribute to the wisdom and experience required for us to create the specific policy planks of The DayLight Movement.

The interests of the minority in any particular situation will be safeguarded with the assistance of an empowered "truth squad," consisting of the mainstream press, bloggers, and the DayLight Movement itself. We-the-People will make the decisions that our elected and appointed officials will execute, and which we will know they can execute because of their proven expertise. We-the-People are looking for men and women of principle. Here is our checklist:

- **You must be an honest communicator.** Honesty in politics is requisite for the development of our collective "Master Mind," which will consist of individual citizens, an ombudsman-oriented Congress, and the lobbyists and interest groups who will be focusing their persuasive efforts on We-the-People. Only truthful communication will enable us to accomplish our goals. Courage and the willingness to admit one's mistakes is something to be admired and applauded. No longer passive victims of government, if you are honest with us We-the-People will be with you all the way. We promise not to confuse "flip-flopping" with the wisdom of flexibility and adaptability for the common good; attributes that the current administration and our military sorely lack.

- **Leaders do the right things; managers do things right.** Know which you are and why. If you are a candidate for Chief Executive then, instead of offering us a platform, we will give you one that we will help you to develop at the DayLight Forum and expect you to execute. This is a prime differentiator between the old ways and the new direct initiative/referendum method described herein. The president's job is to: publicly establish a national culture that incorporates all of us; define the values of that culture; and then do everything in his or her power to reflect and enforce them. All other elected and administrative offices are responsible for providing you and us with the best and most complete information possible in order for us to make solid decisions that support your defined mission.

- **Ability trumps charisma.** The campaign for the presidency of the greatest and most powerful nation on earth should not be a folksy popularity or likeability contest. Being photogenic matters only in Hollywood. In a DayLight government, substance trumps form every time. Just as the private sector hires the best candidate for a particular job, not the best campaigner or fundraiser, we will not elect the leader of the free world based on superficial qualities and vague positions on important issues.

> **"You cannot be leading if you are misleading."**
> *Zbigniew Brezinski*

One of the major challenges that We-the-People currently face is that of bringing our government into the 21st century. It took the election of a president who has stupidly and deceitfully led us into a valley of hatred and disrespect in the eyes of the world, and into an economic environment that purports to be healthy when literally millions are out of work or worse, in order for us to be sufficiently motivated to make the kind of change being advocated here. The scariest part of it all is that George W. Bush actually believes his handler's lies. That may sound harsh but this is personal for all of us regardless of our political persuasion. Whether he did it dishonestly or just plain recklessly, Bush's amateurism needlessly caused the injury and death of thousands of American soldiers and untold damage to their families. The aggregate financial and social toll on our nation will not be known for decades, and the damage done in the eyes of the rest of the world will surely last for a century or more. Anyone who thinks otherwise need only look at the legacy we created 58 years ago in Palestine, and 40 years ago in Vietnam.

> **"As democracy is perfected, the office of president represents, more and more closely, the inner soul of the people. On some great and glorious day the plain folks of the land will reach their heart's desire at last and the White House will be adorned by a downright moron."** *H.L. Mencken, July 26, 1920*

The two-term presidency of George W. Bush is instructive of how money can put into office someone who has proven to be so destructive to an entire nation. Bush's coterie of Big Money handlers caused a "coronation by checkbook" in 2000, and a second one by fear and lies in 2004. Essentially, those who contributed $125 million to the 2004 Bush campaign installed someone who has cost us $1 Trillion; 2,700 dead soldiers, 18,000 maimed, and a loss of respect around the world.

It is more than a little telling that the fear generated by an unjust and uncalled for war caused us to reelect a president who few people like or respect. Yet, if we judged George W. Bush by his accomplishments as a father, a Yale University graduate, an MBA, a former governor of one of our largest states, an oil man, a sports team owner, and a major political fundraiser, we would have to place him in the top 1% of the nation in terms of success. But was he really the best that We-the-People could put forth as the leader of the free world? Many of his major life accomplishments are either lies (the resurrection of the Texas educational system, and his military service); bought (the Texas governorship, the Texas Rangers baseball team, and the presidency); or someone else's doing (virtually every idea that he has floated in the course of his political career). In short, other than privatizing Social Security, the man has had few, if any, original or truly "presidential" ideas.

Bush continues to provide proof of his incompetence in the form of his political appointments, such as that of Condoleeza Rice (a proven liar) to the post of Secretary of State. In the line of succession, Rice is three heartbeats away from the presidency! A failure as National Security Advisor, her confirmation as Secretary of State should motivate all of us to rise up against a political system that permits such a travesty to occur. She lied during her tenure as National Security Advisor and, when she was called on it during her 2005 confirmation hearing for Secretary of State, she responded by telling the questioner that she resented having her credibility questioned. A ballsy, but transparent response, that is characteristic of the hubris that pervades the Bush gang. In January of 2005, *Common Cause* reported that:

> "Rep. Joel Hefley (R-CO) was ousted today as chairman of the House Ethics Committee. In replacing Hefley, House Speaker Dennis Hastert (R-IL) is sending a clear signal that partisan politics trumps accountability and ethical standards in the "people's House." Rep. Hefley led an Ethics Committee that took difficult steps in investigating and ultimately admonishing House Majority Leader Tom DeLay (R-TX) for unethical behavior three separate times last year. Today, Rep. Hefley's leadership is being tossed aside as an apparent punishment for having the chutzpah to stand up to DeLay and carry out his duty as Ethics Committee Chairman honorably."

DeLay's ethical crisis has brought yet more dishonor to the House leadership, which felt compelled to remove someone (Hefley) who actually believed in upholding ethical standards. For further proof that hypocrisy and loss of values have become commonplace in our hallowed halls of government, and that it is polluting even the best in Congress, one only need look to Senator John McCain: an otherwise good and honest man who prostituted himself at the 2004 Republican National Convention by supporting a man who slandered him. Any rational person would think that, when George W. Bush pulled the same kind of lying smear against presidential candidate John

Kerry, Senator McCain would have had the character to speak up rather than cop out. It is a sign of hope for our society that the public seems to have caught on to his disingenuous act as evidenced by the "cold shoulder" he received while delivering commencement addresses at two universities in May of this year (2006).

"A tyrant must put on the appearance of uncommon devotion to religion. Subjects are less apprehensive of illegal treatment from a ruler whom they consider god-fearing and pious... they do less easily move against him, believing that he has the gods on his side."
Aristotle

President Bush's claim to be a prayerful man of God is a smokescreen that grows thinner with each gust of ineptness, as well as with the gradual uncovering of lies about everything from who Dick Cheney secretly met with to formulate energy policy (one of whom was Enron's Chairman, the late Ken Lay), to why thousands of American soldiers are being sent as cannon fodder to a needless war.

In his second inaugural speech, the President called for the United States to spread democracy throughout the world: *"Only one force is strong enough to break through hatred and tyranny,"* he said, *"and that is the force of human freedom."* A good idea, Mr. President, but only if it is spread by example and encouragement, not forced down sovereign nations' throats. Before we embark on a mission to spread democracy throughout the world, we need to clean up our own democracy. America may very well have the best form of government in the world, but who are we to force our notion of what is right on other nations? How many more Americans will have to die overseas in needless combat? How many here at home will go hungry or be denied a proper education while Bush & Co. spend hundreds of billions of no-bid dollars playing God? Now that Bush is a lame duck, there is nothing we can legally do to get rid of this "cowboy," but what we can do is ensure that people like him and his cronies are never again given this much power.

"Charisma is the cloak of both the savior and the charlatan"
Unknown

We, as a nation, need to stop voting for people and start voting for issues, and we need our elected ombudsmen-politicians to discuss these issues, not combat medals or personal peccadilloes. When we elect people for their wisdom and advisory expertise, we will have largely eliminated the penchant for "gotcha" personal attacks, doctored photos, and campaign distortions. The pork, personal corruption, and lies that put us at war and waste our hard-earned dollars provide more than enough evidence that our trusted officials have too much power – power that rightly belongs to We-the-People.

To take back control of our country, we first need to take back control of our money. This process starts with redirecting political contributions into a system based on the DayLight model, rather than into the deep pockets of the corrupt political parties controlled by Big Money and special interests. Our current environment of conflicted politicians puts an unnecessary reality-distortion field between We-the-People and final decisions made on important matters; thereby enabling things like self-serving pork amendments to be tacked on under a dark veil of secrecy.

One of the more egregious examples: In 2004, *The New York Times* published an article entitled "Built With Steel, Perhaps, but Greased With Pork." The following is an excerpt of this article, which reported on the activities of Alaska Senator Ted Stevens and Representative Don Young, Chairman of the House Transportation and Infrastructure Committee:

> "One [bridge], here in Ketchikan, would be among the biggest in the United States: a mile long, with a top clearance of 200 feet from the water – 80 feet higher than the Brooklyn Bridge and just 20 feet short of the Golden Gate Bridge. It would connect this economically depressed, rain-soaked town of 7,845 people to an island that has about 50 residents and the area's airport, which offers six flights a day (a few more in the summer). It could cost about **$200 million** [emphasis added]. As a transportation solution, its own citizens' see the Ketchikan Bridge as something of a joke. It would replace a five-minute ferry crossing.'
>
> The other bridge would span an inlet for nearly two miles to tie Anchorage to a port that has a single regular tenant and almost no homes or businesses. It would cost up to **$2 Billion** [emphasis added].

When asked why a town with one main road, a dwindling population, and virtually nowhere to drive needs a bridge to rival the world's great spans, people here inevitably respond with two words: Don Young. Mr. Young, mindful that the highway bill comes up for renewal only once every six years or so, and that the House Republican Conference imposes three-term limits on committee chairmanships, says the opportunity to pour so many federal dollars into his home state comes once in a lifetime, and should be seized."

After Hurricanes Katrina and Rita there was an embarrassing uproar about the cost of "the bridge to nowhere." In mid-November 2005 Congress "appeared" to have stripped both bridges from its current spending bill but, as reported in *The New York Times* ("G.O.P. Strips Mandatory Funding for Two Alaskan Bridges," November 16, 2005) a closer inspection shows that, "Alaska will still receive the money that had been set aside for the bridges to spend as it likes on transportation needs" and that the two bridges "... could still be built but now must compete with other transportation funding priorities in the state." Once a little time has passed, do you really think that these egregious examples of pork won't be reactivated in all their porcine glory? Mark my words: This purported withdrawal is merely a hiatus until the proverbial coast is clear. Congress may not be able to pass a decent Medicare bill for years and years, but they seem to move quite swiftly when it comes to "pork products" like the Ketchikan and Anchorage Bridges.

This Alaskan boondoggle is a classic example of a local issue that needs to be decided nationally because *it's our money.* Consider this: according to *Edutopia Magazine* ("High School's New Face," November 2004"), "In 2003, $4 Billion was spent on high school construction." We could build a lot of schools for the cost of a ridiculous $2 Billion bridge that even pragmatic Alaskans are deriding in town hall meetings and in the press, asserting that it will actually make travel more difficult. A previously stated sentiment bears repeating here: *"power in the hands of the federal government is not the problem, misuse of that power and misapplication of our money by conflicted politicians is the problem."*

The power that pork-mongers like Alaska's Ted Stevens and Don Young wield over our hard-earned money will be removed when We-the-People take that power back. Only when we eliminate our elected leader's penchant for greed and avarice will we be able to run our nation's financial affairs like a business that must produce a profit each year, instead of permitting them to treat our treasury like a bottomless personal piggy bank and means to buy votes.

"Pork" is not entirely the fault of our elected officials. Constitutional historian, Alan Hirsch, points out that "Congress' seniority system gives voters in every district a disincentive to remove their incumbent: A new representative generally translates into less pork for the district. The result, at times, is what economists call a 'collective action' problem: Everyone wants to throw the bums out, but most vote to keep their own bum in."

> **"When the people find they can vote themselves money, that will herald the end of the republic."** *Benjamin Franklin*

Our elected leaders are literally spending us into poverty. If they were held to the same criteria that they voted for in Sarbanes-Oxley*, they would be in jail. Can you see why we need to act quickly?

* Sarbanes-Oxley: a massively misguided, knee-jerk, overkill attempt to ensure much-needed accurate reporting of corporate financial performance.

SEEK FIRST TO UNDERSTAND, THEN TO BE UNDERSTOOD:

The path to a better America will not be an easy one to forge. We can no longer count on some photogenic father figure or "aircraft carrier Rambo" to lead us out of our troubles and into a brighter future. We live in a world that is being torn apart by madmen and corporate criminals, and if we want to save America we cannot passively educate ourselves simply by reading newspapers and watching the nightly news. We must earnestly and honestly talk to each other; we must learn about the world around us and figure out what is needed to make it better. This will require an unbiased information database and public forum, as well as a public education system that teaches us how to learn and *how* to interact with each other.

> **"Leadership and learning are indispensable to each other."**
> *John F. Kennedy speech prepared for delivery in Dallas the day of his assassination, November 22, 1963*

We-the-People have two choices: we can become students who take an active role in our government or we can:

- Be "victims" and lose our pensions to "corporate pigs" who can't live on $10 million salaries;
- Lose our health insurance while our employers report record earnings;
- Lose our pensions to corporate scofflaws who strip our corporate employer's assets, reaping billions of dollars that belong to us;
- Lose our homes to unemployment because no one has an original idea about how to sustainably reinvigorate our national productivity in a manner that actually employs us;
- Lose our lives in wars that should not be fought; and
- Permit our air, ground and water to be poisoned and then let the corporate perpetrators off the hook for cleanup.

There are so many ways to become victims of the very people who we elect to care for and protect America. Our collective efforts at the DayLight Forum will blaze a path to real change.

Experience tells us that whether you're talking about a business or a country, if you want to find out what's really needed, don't hire $2,500 per day consultants or elect politicians who soon fall out-of-touch. If you really want to know "what's broke and how to fix it," ask the people who are actually doing the work and living in the real world. That's what I did. This book is a just the beginning of an effort to organize that raw information – *our insights about what's really needed* – into a coherent plan and platform for positive change – a DayLight Forum led by those who can best do the job no matter what it may be.

You don't have to listen to profane, cop-killer, rap lyrics or see the latest movies to ascertain how far America's values, sense of fairness and basic decency have slipped. One needs to look no further than to corporate America and our mainstream press. A prime example of both is the press hailing as "perhaps the greatest corporate leader of our time," a publicly acknowledged adulterer who, while CEO of a Fortune 50 corporation, refused to remove literally tons of chemical poison that his company deposited on the bottom of the Hudson River, and then reportedly aided and abetted the disguising of literally tens of millions of dollars in retirement perks on top of the riches he reaped while in power; or a former president, who lied about an adulterous affair when he didn't need to. Both are brilliant men who command six-figure speaking fees from a fawning corporate America. Do you think this is missed by our children or by young adults entering the workplace?

Our Congress and President display an ever-compromising set of values that have no credibility. In a news article published by, *The New York Times* ("Pressure Mounting to Ensure Ethical Behavior in the House" March 21, 2004) Fred Wertheimer, president of the group, Democracy 21, was quoted as saying, "When you don't have any real enforcement process, you live in the Wild West and people do what they want." The Times went on to report that, "Leaders of both parties oppose the change [in the complaint process]." It was only after a loud and long protest by We-the-People that Congress backed down on its plan to drastically limit the ability to police itself. Even so, Congress remains a place of temptation and a conduit to corporate largess rather than an honest forum for We-the-People.

In an article titled "Ethics Office For Hill Rejected – Bipartisan Defeat For Independent Lobbying Overseer" (March 3, 2006) *Washington Post* Staff Writer Jeffrey H. Birnbaum reported that, "A Senate committee yesterday rejected a bipartisan proposal to establish an independent office to oversee the enforcement of congressional ethics and lobbying laws, signaling a reluctance in Congress to beef up the enforcement of its rules on lobbying." On March 29, by a vote of 60 to 37, the Senate formally voted to kill the proposal.

Humorous approaches, outraged approaches, trivializing approaches – all have been tried in an attempt to address the way we are governed, how we conduct ourselves as a nation, and how we are perceived by the world. But no one is coming up with any hard proposals about how to actually take back control of our country and our destiny; this book and The DayLight Forum do precisely that. Instead of inane, talking-head news announcers and talk show hosts avidly discussing political mud-slinging and issues that have nothing to do with the true challenges that we face, We-the-People will have a public forum – the DayLight Movement – that actually accomplishes something. Instead of talking about people and parties, we will be talking about ideas.

"Simple minds talk about people, average minds talk about events, and great minds talk about ideas." *Anonymous*

We-the-People need to get on the same page. This does not mean that we all have to think alike. We just need to scrap this "us against them" mentality that lies at the heart of the American political party system. It is nice to think that we can elect a principled and charismatic leader who can make a difference, but the reality is that, no matter who is elected under our current system, they are dominated by a coterie of handlers who take their orders from the Big Money lobbyists that represent the dark side of our nation's military-industrial complex. Politicians and their handlers rely heavily on pollsters for insight as to just how far they can push the voters. Unfortunately, polls can be twisted to provide whatever information those in power want to hear. A true referendum system, alone or combined with a DayLight Forum "national heat map," can provide a cleaner, more accurate and fully disclosed real-time poll of what we really want.

Just because you do not take an interest in politics doesn't mean politics won't take an interest in you. *Pericles (430 B.C.)*

TAKING CHARGE

If you believe the adage "the Lord helps those who help themselves," then you are subscribing to the concept of a world of free will: one where God prefers to let us grow by working through our own problems and challenges. It is time for us to abandon the mindset that we need experts to decide domestic or foreign policy; we need them to *advise* us. We-the-People are not infants incapable of understanding what is best for our nation and for us. For the current "establishment of experts," who we call "Congress," to think otherwise is to denigrate their own ability to communicate and educate. Under our current system, they have no incentive to do either. When corrupt or just plain inept politicians are no longer senselessly revered as authority figures and experts who "know what is best for us better than we do," their ability to sway our opinion with cheap rhetoric, fear, and lies will be supplanted by the light of full disclosure. The power to shape our destiny is now in our hands. Sound arguments, not false authoritarian image, will carry the day. As noted peace proponent and editor of *Tikkun Magazine,* Rabbi Michael Lerner put it:

"There is no one alive on the planet who doesn't bear some part of the responsibility for the craziness that manifests itself in lack

of justice, kindness, generosity, peace and love. On the social and political level, we've all allowed the world to get out of hand. Every decision we make to leave it to others, either because we are too satisfied with our lives to bother about the suffering of others, or too certain of the inevitability of the fruitlessness of our political efforts, is a decision which helps make the world the way we say we don't want it to be."

We-the-People must establish an all-American platform for the next four years, which candidates vying for the job of president must fulfill. Just as no investor in his or her right mind would invest in a company that will not disclose its management team until after their investment has been made so, too, the people should be entitled to full disclosure. Presidential candidates will be required to identify their Cabinet choices *prior* to election. Below cabinet level, instead of administrative positions being filled by appointees, we will create a process to *qualify and hire* the most qualified person for each position. After all, this is *our government and our lives* that we are talking about.

A LESS THAN SUPREME COURT

"The Supreme Court is not the ultimate authority for constitutional interpretation. It is subservient to the People, who can amend the Constitution through a kind of national referendum."
Akhil Amar and Alan Hirsch.

Even our United States Supreme Court, the highest court in the land, has been compromised. It is no longer a living embodiment of "a balanced scale of justice." Instead, it intrudes into the legislative and executive branches more deeply than is called for by the concept of Checks and Balances. The Supreme Court also intrudes into our personal privacy far deeper than is necessary. Instead of reflecting the values and mores of We-the-People, candidates for appointment pander to the left or right leanings of whoever happens to be in office when there is a vacancy.

If ever there were a reason to take back our court system and our democracy it is in the example currently being set in early 2006 by South Dakota's challenge to Roe vs. Wade. Despite the fact that the majority of Americans support abortion rights, a man who has been described by members of both major parties as perhaps the most inept president in the history of our country is stacking the Court with people who will strike down our collective, democratic, will. In a March 12, 2006 editorial ("A Warning from South Dakota") *The New York Times* reported that:

> "[abortion opponents] have also begun predicting that Justice John Paul Stevens, the oldest member, will leave the court, allowing President Bush to appoint another anti-Roe justice... Roe ushered in three decades of complacency for the majority of Americans who support abortion rights. South Dakota's harsh new law is a clear sign that the time for complacency is over."

Yet another example of why we need to take our country back from the courts, as well as from a conflicted Congress, is the Supreme Court's outrageous decision (8-0) on March 21, 2006 making it all but impossible for individual investors to join forces to file fraud lawsuits against companies that have demonstrably committed specific fraud. This obscene ruling was handed down despite the fact that a group of Merrill Lynch stock brokers wanted to join the shareholder suit because they, too, were mislead by their firm's analysts who privately characterized stocks that they recommended as a "disaster" or "dog." Somehow the fact that Merrill Lynch was fined $100 million for this fraud was not evidence enough to persuade the Court that injured investors should be able to band together to bring a legal claim that would be prohibitively expensive for an individual to bring. Merrill can pay a $100 million fine as easily as if it were a tip on a lunch tab. Justice John Paul Stevens opined that to rule otherwise would allow "... wasteful, duplicative litigation.... The magnitude of the federal interest in protecting the integrity and efficient operation of the market for nationally traded securities cannot be overstated." Unless I'm missing something, it sounds like the Court caved into Big Money.

Let's "cut to the chase" with a simple but effective and logical solution: elect Supreme Court justices like we do judges of lower courts. Why should our highest court be subject to the appointment whims of a Big-Money-bought politician who may not have his constituents' best interests at heart? Why are we allowing the Supreme Court to be formed by someone who is not qualified to discern, much less select, the level of excellence required of a Supreme Court justice? Bush's failed choice of crony Harriet Miers is a prime example. She may very well be a fine lawyer and citizen, but when members of both dominant political parties derided her intellectual qualifications, what does that say about the man who nominated her? Electing our Supreme Court justices will remove the specter of influence by Big Money and special interests, just like it will with the ombudsmen-politicians who we elect. The less we have to rely on someone else's motives and fealty to the highest bidder, the more assured we can be that our individual quality-of-life, our collective well-being, and our country's destiny will have the best chance of long-term survival and success.

To those who claim that creating a realistic presidential platform, improving the timing and speed of identification and selection of cabinet and administrative personnel, and cleaning up the Supreme Court will be too arduous and cumbersome a task, I ask: what better task can we perform than that of setting our government straight? What would happen if our military let privates become generals overnight, simply because they had the right connections?

Once this governmental vetting process is done for the first time, subsequent job fillings will come much easier. In fact, by eliminating or at least greatly reducing partisanship and patronage, our system will have markedly surer quality and continuity. Then we will truly know that those who we put in leadership and management positions are qualified to explain, inform, and educate us so that we can vote intelligently. The appellations "government worker" and "government official" will, once again, be terms of honor and prestige.

While it will take much thought and research, we can even create a means to rapidly but fairly remove "bad actors" by a vote of no-confidence. Part of our new Checks and Balances will be an ombudsman to watch the ombudsmen we elect. An unofficial but essential part of this watchdog system will be the previously mentioned new social phenomenon known as "the blogger community." A prime, if not the best, example of a political blog and blog power is Daily Kos (http://www.dailykos.com) started 4 years ago by Markos Moulitsas Zúniga; a true pioneer and inspirational leader in the political blogosphere. I feel sheepish even mentioning Markos and Daily Kos because he and his Left-oriented but fair-and-balanced Website are so popular that most of you likely already know about them. Moreover, because, there are so many other good blogs and politically oriented Websites, if I start to list more than *The Daily Kos*, I won't know where to stop. So I will take a pass on creating a massive list here and rely on those of you who become "Friends of DayLight" volunteers to help build a quality link list at the DayLight Forum Website.

The Daily Kos is living proof of what can be accomplished by a dedicated core of passionate Americans. According to Matt Bai, a contributing writer for *The New York Times* Magazine, ("Can Bloggers Get Real?" May 28, 2006), "With some 600,000 visitors a day, Daily Kos reaches more Americans – albeit like-minded Americans – than all but a handful of the largest daily newspapers." The first of what portends to be an annual gathering of a thousand or more Americans, called the "Yearly Kos," took place in Las Vegas the first week of June, 2006. Clearly the American public is looking to step out of the rut of apathy and to find a way to "move the ball" of life.

The primary difference between Daily Kos and the DayLight Forum is that we are neither Left or Right; we are purposely all-encompassing with a mission to, as President John F. Kennedy advised, **"Let us not seek the Republican answer or the Democratic answer, but the right answer."** To borrow a computer industry term, think of us as a kind of political "GUI" (Graphical User Interface) overlaying *all* political parties with a means to collect, unite, and put into action the best ideas and the best people regardless of party affiliation or no party affiliation.

The bottom line is this: nothing less will do other than a fundamental appraisal and overhaul of our national value system, as well as our method of choosing and monitoring the right leaders to guide us into an increasingly complex future. Let us make our governing process one that welcomes sincere differences of opinion, while also recognizing that we are all in the same boat. Let there be no more hubris, egotism and partisan squabbling among our leaders. The American people need and deserve strong men and women, not petty children, to guide us into the 21st century.

CHAPTER 3

INTERNET VOTING

Before we delve into this intriguing, highly controversial, subject I confess that I have no idea whether some of the initiatives presented for discussion here and throughout this book will prove to be practical. Nor do I have a complete, end-to-end, understanding of how they can best be executed. What I do know is that, among the readers of this book and the people who will come to the DayLight Forum, we will have all the experience and intellectual horsepower needed to bring literally any good idea to life.

Choosing "the best-of-the-best" will be greatly facilitated by the ease with which we can cast our votes. The purest form of government is a system that does not distort or subvert our choices. We-the-People are living in a technology savvy America, and it is time that we seriously consider Internet voting as a viable option along with conventional polling-place and mail-in voting. In addition to providing a conflict-of-interest-free, clear, straight line between the voter and the issue to be decided, direct democracy voting via the Internet will also lower the barrier to participation for many Americans. But before that can happen, serious questions about security and privacy must be answered. It will do no good to have a system that gives all of us a real-time say in governmental matters if our vote can be hijacked.

Many great minds and organizations are working on the challenge of making Internet voting safe and secure. **Accenture** – a global management consulting, technology services, and outsourcing company – is one of a number of organizations leading the way with technological innovation and numerous Internet-based government initiatives that are in successful operation throughout the world. Surely, if we can put a person on the moon, we should be able to figure out how to make Internet voting secure. While this book is not an adequate venue for a detailed description of possible solutions to the challenge of safeguarding our vote over the Internet, four basic suggestions can be made now and then expanded as we continue our dialogue at the DayLight Forum:

1) Provide a password to each voter;

2) Perform random sampling checks to confirm that a particular person voted and how. Direct mailing list companies have been doing this for 50 years;

3) Employ Internet feedback technology that can tell whether a vote is coming from an individual, a machine, or from a central source (this capability already exists and is in use daily by literally thousands of business Websites);

4) Make the penalty for vote fraud life in prison without parole.

Internet voting may very well turn out to be less of a problem than the current mess over antiquated mechanical voting machines and touch screens, both of which can be rigged as easily as an Internet vote could be compromised. Can whatever damage hackers could do to an Internet-based voting system be any worse than what happened in Florida in the year 2000, and in Ohio in 2004? If we can make debit and credit card transactions secure, we can certainly secure one of our most precious rights as Americans.

The objectives of The DayLight Movement can be accomplished without Internet voting; but, when questions regarding security are resolved, Internet voting would vastly increase our ability to take part in a markedly richer national dialogue. In the meantime we will have the weight of a united voice – i.e., that national "heat map" that I mentioned earlier – at the DayLight Forum where politicians will be unable to ignore us. Despite the challenges that it poses, the democratic power of an Internet-based voting system is simply too promising for us to give up on it.

E-voting will be the front end of an e-government system that will speed up delivery of information and services, as well as ensure that our voices resonate, not just at election time but all the time. As David R. Hunter, former Global Managing Partner of the Accenture Government Practice, stated in his article, "The Role of Government in The Age of Knowledge" *(Accenture Insights, May 2000):*

> "Open, transparent, responsive government has never been in greater demand nor more achievable... Access to information is no longer restricted or expensive... With the click of a mouse, citizens and businesses can provide feedback on a service, participate in an advisory committee, or request a performance summary."

Paraphrasing further from Mr. Hunter's insights: instead of having our current 200-year old patchwork of policies and systems housed in vertical and often isolated agencies, with delivery of services that do not meet our needs or expectations, we will have an integrated and open system that permits a clear path from concept to delivery.

This kind of thing is happening all over the world. From Ireland to Singapore to Ohio, governments have a vision of transforming their country or state into intelligent systems where technology is prevalent at home and at work, linking government, businesses, schools, and households in *an environment of openness* where decisions and policies are made in the light of day.

By being accountable and allowing citizen stakeholders to participate in decision-making, measurement and feedback, governments and citizens alike have the opportunity to quickly and accurately gauge the information and advice that they receive and the value of what they create. Can you think of a better way to engender confidence in our government than to permit its people to hold the voting reins of an open-book (not "open checkbook") system? We will have a government that is open 24 hours a day, 7 days a week – a government that is responsive to the point of being organic and that displays the following characteristics:

- **Dynamic open-book connections** that provide integrated and comprehensive touch points between government and its constituent's daily lives;
- **Policy speed-to-market** – radically accelerating policy formulation and implementation in order to improve results;
- **Well-engaged, knowledgeable, constituents** as integral stake holders in the success of government processes and outcomes.
- **Accountability and measurability** will be more attainable and more accurate than at any time in the history of the world.

AN OPPORTUNITY TO SERVE OUR COUNTRY AND MAKE HISTORY

An exciting prospect for **DayLight Members** (also known as **"Friends of DayLight"**) is the opportunity to use the DayLight Forum as our nation's first truly functional Internet voting lab. If we are going to use the Forum to debate and straw vote on matters that are important to us, why not use the Internet and the first three voting safeguards, listed previously, as a "beta test" for an eventual national Internet voting system? Because we are widely dispersed geographically, and will be voting in large enough numbers to be statistically relevant, we can invite Internet voting tech and engineering proponents to work with us to accelerate perfection of a truly workable national voting system.

PART TWO:
DOMESTIC POLICY

CHAPTER 4

THE ECONOMY

"Virtually everything is under federal control nowadays except the federal budget." *Herman E. Talmadge*

What We-the-People really like about our democracy is not our current representative format, but rather the freedom we enjoy – a freedom that is being eroded in tandem with the draining of our economy. Naysayers who ridicule such an assertion need look no further than the holders of the majority of our national debt: Japan, the Saudis, and the rising giant China. Proverbs 22:7 sums it up nicely: *"The rich ruleth over the poor, and the borrower is servant to the lender."* At our present rate of reckless spending, which currently exceeds what we earn as a nation annually, the realization of this proverb draws ever closer. Whether we're talking about a country or an individual, spend more than you make and eventually you will become bankrupt.

Our current political system has weakened us as a nation and as a people, both spiritually and economically. The elected leaders who we look to for guidance are the ones getting us into trouble by putting the interests of the banking industry lobby ahead of the interests of their constituents. Our elected officials have permitted the promotion of loose credit laws without demanding that our schools do a better job of educating our young people about the insidious, heroin-like dangers of easy credit, which have gotten so many into serious trouble. We have become reliant on political "rock stars" to solve economic problems that they are neither qualified nor particularly disposed to cure.

We-the-People need to take back our economy and put skilled professionals in position to inform and guide us, so we can do what is best for us, not for a banking industry and healthcare industry that gouge us at every turn. Complexity and overspending are what got us into our current multi-trillion dollar mess; we need the best minds to guide us out. Note that I did not say, "lead" us out – I said, "guide." Under the DayLight Movement, all of us are responsible for working together toward a solution to our economic challenges so that all of us, not just some of us, can survive and thrive. Every other form of government and economic management that's ever been tried has eventually become corrupted, but then no other form of government has ever been proposed to be conducted so totally in the bright light of day.

ASLEEP AT THE SWITCH

Our lack of creativity is killing us. We-the-People want to know where the real job creation ideas are. Who was "asleep at the switch" as economic reality made it clear that, in order to remain competitive, our major corporate employers would have to outsource many jobs to lower-paying foreign labor forces? Who, among the politicians who voted for NAFTA (The North American Free Trade Agreement), had the foresight to plan for a major financial and sociological transition caused by the loss of a major portion of our manufacturing industry? The free trade fiasco is a classic example of a deadly combination of Big Money interests and Congress' failure to focus on the needs of American workers.

Like water seeking its own level, free trade is likely inevitable because business always seeks the lowest bidder. Our elected officials cannot do much about that, but these so-called experts certainly could have prepared our nation for the drastic loss of jobs here at home. They are like many inexperienced teenagers: no linear projection or planning, no sense of consequences. Their answer to any problem is to spend their way out of it. The American worker deserves better.

If one good thing has come out of the tragedy of an immoral invasion of Iraq, and from the hurricane disasters of 2005, it is the realization that even the most powerful nation on earth can spend itself into financial and human resource bankruptcy. The lowering of interest rates by the Federal Reserve is our government's pat answer to the question of how to ameliorate brutal conditions caused by an unemployment picture that, like an iceberg, has far more jagged dangers lying just below its surface. Perhaps we would not be in our current economic rut if our business and elected leaders stopped focusing on the short term and lying to themselves about the consequences of global political, economic, and climatic change and started looking at new ways to remain on the top rung of the competitive ladder.

The fact that we are rapidly becoming a consumer economy rather than a producer economy and the resultant damage to our economic security and standing in the world does not fully show yet because the rest of the world still wants to get into "the land of the free." But as democracy and varying forms of capitalism flourish elsewhere, that psychological advantage will evaporate as people look for greener or equally green pastures outside the United States. We need to bring in advisors who can see "the big picture" while it is still small. We must creatively and intelligently accelerate our evolution into a new kind of world leader or those who envy our standard of living will overtake us. To paraphrase Tom Peters and Robert Waterman from their book, *In Search of Excellence:* "The railroad companies could have owned the airline industry if they had recognized that they were in the *transportation* business, not the locomotive business." As a nation we must start thinking beyond short term, quarterly driven, economic boundaries.

The greatest nation in the world has become reactive instead of proactive in the face of massive, geometrically accelerating, global change. A classic example: how did we miss the fact that the awesome population growth and rate of industrialization in both China and India would soon force us into a bidding war for a dwindling world oil supply? Why have we not built a new oil refinery in the United States in the past 30 years? The oil shortage that occurred after hurricanes Katrina and Rita is due more to our lack of refining capacity than it is to the Middle East's and Canada's (our biggest supplier, by the way) inability to pump oil faster. Why have our leaders – the people who we trust with our children's future – not instituted a massive technological push for alternative energy sources to replace oil? Where are the economic incentives for the R&D required to perfect these alternatives? If we had a simpler tax code, like the one offered in the next chapter, the need for such R&D tax incentives might even be precluded or greatly reduced.

A common theme of virtually every U.S. trade issue is the fact that there is little or no foresight, no real world "what if?" thinking and linear planning about what are often obviously discernible ramifications of each trade decision. The wisdom and planning capability is out there in America and available but there is no reliable way for those who have it to convey it to those in Washington who think that they and their financial masters have all the answers. Dropping import quotas is a prime example: we let China come in and pick our pocket to the tune of billions of dollars by dumping their subsidized goods, then we compounded that error by not reacting quickly enough. A combination of currency manipulation of the yen by China and the elimination of export quotas is wreaking havoc on our economy and on the well-being of our workforce. The same can be said for what it is doing to the Europeans but, due to our diminished standing in the court of world opinion, even that is not enough to get them to unite in a boycott of Chinese goods until China starts playing by the rules of the club that it so badly wants to join. According to the online journal, *China Post,* "China's exports to the United States exceeded its U.S. imports by U.S. $93.5 Billion in the second half of 2004. That trade imbalance was up from U.S. $70.2 Billion in the second half of 2003." Over all, China's trade surplus with the United States was $162 Billion in 2004: a 30.6% increase since 2003, and the United States' largest bilateral deficit.

In January 2005, right under our very noses, our myopic government hosted a major trade show – China Brand 2005 – promoting trade with a country that illegally co-opts our brands with knock-off, bootleg, products costing us an estimated $30 Billion per year in actual lost cash, not to mention lost jobs. Unemployment and a poor economy typically go hand-in-hand. A weak economy encourages borrowing. And who holds most of our national debt in the form of Treasuries? Answer: China.

We are in such a precarious financial position that, even if we could persuade China to not illegally subsidize and dump their goods into our market, not to use slave labor, and to let their currency float on the open market, it would be a disaster because China's products would not be as competitive. This would result in less cash for China to purchase our bonds, which would drive up the interest rates that our Treasury Department has to pay in order to quench our inexhaustible thirst for more of the world's capital. Higher interest means higher borrowing costs for U.S. manufacturers who then must pass that increase onto their customers. In addition to taking more out of our wallets it also makes the cost of our goods less appealing to other countries. We need to turn inward and focus on saving our own country and people for, while we are sticking our noses where we do not belong, China is spending its capital on infrastructure and becoming even more competitive. Our leaders have put us in a vicious no-win cycle. We-the-People are the only ones who can pull us out of it.

EVERYTHING STARTS WITH A DECISION

Our soaring national deficit did not come about solely because of a tax cut or because of an imbalance of trade with the rest of the world; it is there because of reckless, unaccountable spending. The soaring costs of a useless war, and unnecessary government bureaus and programs are sucking a tremendous amount of money out of our lives, our future, and our children's future. Money is being wasted on politically biased decisions made by so-called experts who think that the greatest nation on earth has an infinite amount of financial slack. The numbers have gotten so big that those in Washington can no longer comprehend them so, like an alcoholic, they just keep chugging in hopes that they can block out the pain. How can We-the-People begin to sort through the thousands of expenditures and programs that our congressional representatives deal with (or simply ignore) on a daily basis? The answer is, "One step at a time, the first of which is to *simplify.*"

> **"Before we give you billions more, we want to know what you've done with the trillion you've got."** *Les Aspin*

A primary question that every for-profit business is required to answer must be asked over and over again by our government: *"Will this decision contribute to our profitability and efficiency?"* Note we are not asking if it will contribute to the "betterment of our society;" a phrase that has become a codeword and excuse for reckless spending to gratify the short-term political needs of a limited number of people. A prime example is the previously described phenomenon called "pork." Instead of putting our future in the hands of these wasteful "experts," We-the-People must become educated about what is going on in the world. Let our Congressional ombudsmen and the lobbyists bring their best advice and arguments into the light of day, and We-the-People will judge. When this happens the lobbyists win, conservatives win, liberals win, and the press wins, because all become part of the cleaning and sorting process. This is a far wiser approach than our current decision-making process.

The writing is on the wall. In addition to losing the moral high ground in the court of world opinion, America is also in danger of losing its preeminent status as a world financial power, or at least of being matched by up-and-comers like China. We had better get our political, moral, and financial ducks in a row or we will find ourselves in the same fix as an overconfident boxer who, in the opening seconds of the very first round, is stunned by a better-prepared opponent and unable to shift gears and reclaim his dominance.

Fresh solutions are not likely to come from our two dominant political parties, which have, themselves, become special interest groups. They no longer represent the interests of the people because they're too busy raising campaign war chests and fighting each other while trying to survive a growing public perception that they are, at best, an anachronism and, at worst, an impediment to the course of social and human development.

"A politician thinks of the next election - a statesman, of the next generation." *James Freeman Clarke*

CHAPTER 5

TAXES AND TAXATION

"The Declaration of Independence, the words that launched our nation: 1,300 words. The Bible, the word of God: 773,000 words. The Tax Code, the words of politicians: 7,000,000 words – and growing!" *Steve Forbes*

Accounts Receivable Tax
Building Permit Tax
Capital Gains Tax
CDL license Tax
Cigarette Tax
Corporate Income Tax
Court Fines (indirect taxes)
Dog License Tax
Federal Income Tax
Federal Unemployment Tax (FUTA)
Fishing License Tax
Food License Tax
Fuel permit tax
Gasoline Tax (42¢/gallon)
Hunting License Tax
Inheritance Tax
Interest expense (tax on the money)
Inventory tax
IRS Interest Charges (tax on tax)
IRS Penalties (tax on tax)
Liquor Tax
Local Income Tax
Luxury Taxes
Marriage License Tax
Medicare Tax
Property Tax
Real Estate Tax
Septic Permit Tax
Service Charge Taxes
Social Security Tax
Road Usage Taxes (Truckers)
Sales Taxes
Recreational Vehicle Tax
Road Toll Booth Taxes
School Tax
State Income Tax
State Unemployment Tax (SUTA)
Telephone federal excise tax
Telephone federal universal service fee tax
Telephone federal, state and local surcharge taxes
Telephone minimum usage surcharge tax
Telephone recurring and non-recurring charges tax
Telephone state and local tax
Telephone usage charge tax
Toll Bridge Taxes
Toll Tunnel Taxes
Traffic Fines (indirect tax)
Watercraft registration Tax

Trailer registration tax
Utility Taxes
Vehicle License Reg. Tax
Well Permit Tax
Workers Compensation Tax

> **"Not one of these taxes existed 100 years ago and our nation was the most prosperous in the world, had absolutely no national debt, and had the largest middle class in the world. What happened?"** *Anonymous*

> **Politicians are "spending taxpayer money like drunken sailors," and "it's difficult to improve the tax code when government spending is growing three times faster than inflation."**
> *Dan Mitchell, Ph.D. Heritage Foundation*

Our current form of government and financial management has become so complex and bloated that the key to its survival is, to a certain degree, to keep us in the dark of an overwhelming, labyrinthine complexity. Perhaps more than any other, the subject of taxation presents an opportunity for members of both major political parties to voice their universal distaste for a system run amuck.

In October of 2005, President Bush's tax advisory commission recommended alternatives to the current tax plan, neither of which is worth taking the time to read. What is particularly telling is the following quote, as reported in *The New York Times* ("Panel to Urge Bush to Consider 2 Alternative Tax Plans," October 18, 2005): "The panel was instructed to present plans that would raise as much revenue as the current tax system. And in order to raise enough money to abolish the alternative minimum tax, which would generate $1.2 trillion over the next 10 years, the commission had to propose limits on tax breaks."

But why does a new plan have to match today's revenue sum? And why is the commission's alternative plan tied to equalizing the dollar effect of the Alternative Minimum Tax ("ATM") – one of history's dumbest and most ill conceived monstrosities? It is ironic that, in this context, the term ATM refers to *taking* money from you rather than dispensing it. The ATM provides a perfect example of why we have to get rid of the creeps in Congress who spend the people's money like a junkie with a stolen ATM card; the only difference is that this gang has little-to-no fear of getting caught. It is sad to think that this is the same administration whose president, in the wake of Hurricane Katrina, declared that Congress had to cut out unnecessary spending. His statement prompted many rational Americans to wonder why such wasteful spending had not been cut long ago; and why it always seems to take a national disaster on the grandest scale for our government to propose the right measures.

The only difference between a tax man and a taxidermist is that the taxidermist leaves the skin. *Mark Twain*

What we need is an organizational transformation. In this computer age, large, monolithic agencies, like the Internal Revenue Service, are no longer needed to collect money from us. Let's abolish the bloated, overly complex tax code and the IRS bureaucracy, and put its employees into jobs that actually contribute to our gross national product – like the rest of us must do. Let's get the American equivalent of the "Spanish Inquisition" off the backs of hardworking Americans.

"A government which lays taxes on the people not required by urgent public necessity and sound public policy is not a protector of liberty, but an instrument of tyranny." *Calvin Coolidge*

The first wave of DayLight referendums will offer well-thought-out alternatives to our oppressive system of taxation. The two leading candidates are a sales tax (with exclusions for basic living items) and a straightforward head tax.

SALES TAX

I won't take a lot of your time discussing a sales tax only because it us so pervasive in our daily lives that we know what it is and how it works. I will, however, offer a quote in support of a sales tax from Alexander Hamilton, our nation's first Secretary of the Treasury:

"It is a singular advantage of taxes on articles of consumption that they contain in their own nature a security against excess. They prescribe their own limit, which cannot be exceeded without defeating the end proposed -- that is, an extension of the revenue."

HEAD TAX

A head tax system would entail a simple case of division: if you live in America, you pay your fair share of the national budget, as determined by dividing it by the total number of people living in the country. Obviously this number will fluctuate from year to year, but no more than our incomes already do. When people can see a mathematically simple direct correlation between our national budget and what size check they have to write each year, it will motivate and facilitate them to become better educated and more proactive about our national spending. A new social dynamic will come into play, which will make productivity and even our birth rate more predictable, and raise the typical American family demographic to historic heights because both our government and We-the-People will plan, budget and spend realistically. I can think of no other single act that will enable us to balance our budget and to greatly reduce (if not eliminate) things like "pork" spending.

In addition to being the fairest and simplest method of financing our government, a head tax will have a positive effect on over-population. The concept that our land is a never-ending "horn of plenty" that permits us to have more children and naturalize more uneducated, unskilled immigrants than our economy can support is wrongheaded and over. The best way for us to help our brothers and sisters in foreign countries is to get our own act together first. A head tax will help change the culture of our nation from one of "taking" to one where everyone comes up with his or her fair share.

> **"Everyone wants to live at the expense of the state. They forget that the state lives at the expense of everyone."** *Frederic Bastiat*

If we are such a great country, then people should have no problem paying to get in and stay in. No more free rides and no more long-term welfare, especially for immigrants. Legal immigrant or citizen, unless you are medically certified as incapacitated: no welfare, just workfare. This simple social dynamic will improve our nation's financial picture and its productivity.

Another benefit of a simple head tax is that it will preclude virtually all politically inspired vote-jockeying, as our elected officials alternately raise then lower our income taxes, or add new ones to our tax base only to take them away whenever it is politically expedient. The ever-manipulated gasoline tax is a prime example of Congress taxing everything in sight to support their fiscal irresponsibility. An intelligent head tax will not preclude critically needed improvements to our infrastructure; for example, we can still finance roads and bridges with a *limited* gas tax that is tied to a matching tax on the energy companies who basically harvest our natural resources at little-or-no charge and then sell them to us; generating staggering profits in the process. States can still finance things for themselves by charging a commercial real estate tax or their own head tax; perhaps even a sales tax if we let them. If these charges become too onerous, people can either move or vote for change. The important thing is we get to hold on to the money that we earn; we no longer have to spend time and money filing ridiculously torturous tax forms; and we have more of a say as to how our government spends what we do send in each year.

If politicians try to tell us that our national budget is so immense that a simple head tax would fall far short financially, then one can logically conclude that we are spending ourselves into a financial grave. I say this because, whether we do it within our current system or a simple head tax system, at the end of the day we will be writing a check – the only question is "for how much and why?"

For proof of how our current governmental budgetary system is weakening our country, one needs to look no further than the phenomenon of a weakening dollar, which is a direct result of our need to borrow more money to slake a monstrously growing national debt. We're caught up in a yet another vicious cycle where borrowing weakens our dollar and a weakened dollar forces us to borrow more. The pat answer that we get from our politicians is that this issue is too complicated and that only they know how to cure this mess. At least, that is what they have been telling us for the past 50 or so years. But so-called "expertise" will not cure our fiscal challenge – we've tried that. A new system, with a simple checkbook-balancing discipline, guided by knowledgeable Congressional ombudsmen, is the only thing that will cure what ails us.

WE DON'T REALLY HATE THE RICH

An easy target for pandering politicians is to exploit the public's purported jealousy of our wealthy fellow Americans – a cheap attempt to capitalize on a non-existent class warfare. Despite the controversy surrounding taxation of the rich, most Americans do not believe that the wealthiest among us should pay inordinate tax bills. In part this is because, deep down, *we all want to be wealthy* and, if and when that day comes, we do not want to lose that hard-earned money to unnecessary taxation.

A prime example is Congress' spurious defense of the death tax because, "the government would lose so much annual revenue." Just because there would be a significant loss of money, that never should be taken from us in the first place, does not make the death tax right. Apparent Congressional acquiescence to the public outcry over the unfairness of "taxing the dead one more time" is an illusion – a cheap, insulting, and bogus pacifier. Granted, the federal estate tax is scheduled to gradually disappear by 2010 but it is also scheduled to return in 2011 just five years from now when the temporary repeal expires. Any gain at the federal level (however temporary) will be offset when the states take their turn at the feeding trough. If you are looking for an indicator of just how skewed our elected official's values have become consider a government that thinks nothing of taxing something simply because it's an easy target. Sounds like necrophilic robbery to me.

> **"To take from one, because it is thought his own industry and that of his fathers has acquired too much, in order to spare to others, who, or whose fathers, have not exercised equal industry and skill, is to violate arbitrarily the first principle of association – the guarantee to everyone the free exercise of his industry and the fruits acquired by it."** *Thomas Jefferson*

A healthy perspective for us to have about the rich is to acknowledge that, in any free-enterprise society, someone is going to be on top. Instead of attacking people with whom we would like to trade places, we should accept that they are a necessary and positive aspect of a healthy society. Consider: without the rich, there would be no museums, libraries, charitable medical foundations or research centers. The rich create jobs and they spend money on first and second homes, cars, planes, jewelry, and thousands of other essentials and non-essentials that We-the-People make and sell at a profit. The rich provided the financial incentive to develop indoor plumbing, electricity in the home, refrigeration, air conditioning, the telephone and the automobile – all things that We-the-People enjoy, and that many of us take for granted. Remember the first flat-screen HDTVs priced at $14,000 just four years ago? If the affluent had not provided the initial market for technologically innovative products, we would still be watching three channels on 12-inch black-and-white screens. Sure, we all do our best to help, but think about it: in large measure it is the rich who employ and feed the middle-class and the poor.

Because the wealthy are an easy minority to attack, our politicians have been using a "tax the hated rich" ploy as an emotional tool to gain votes. Converting our state and federal Congressmen and women to educators and ombudsmen fighting for the good of all of us will preclude them from lowering themselves by trying to appeal to negative emotions like hate and envy. To those who truly hate or envy the rich: you will be pleased to know that, if we adopt a sales tax system, the rich will pay the most. And, if we adopt a head tax, the issue of what the rich pay becomes moot because we will all pay our *fair share*. In an enlightened environment, like the DayLight Movement, issues like taxation are just another instance of "the bigger the problem, the simpler and more straightforward the solution."

"Calvin Coolidge, one of our most underrated Presidents, put it well:'Our country,' he said, 'was conceived in the theory of local self-government. It has been dedicated by long practice to that wise and beneficent policy. It is the foundation principle of our system of liberty.' When Cal Coolidge was President, taxes -- Federal, State, and local -- were taking a dime out of every dollar earned, and two-thirds of that dime went to State and local government. By 1980 taxes were up to 35 cents of every dollar, and three-fifths of that came to Washington. ... First, we must continue working to return power to levels of government closer to the people. We believe that when it comes to running county government, county officials will always do better from the county seat than bureaucrats could ever do from Washington." *Ronald Reagan*

CHAPTER 6

SOCIAL SECURITY

Social Security – also known as the Old Age, Survivors and Disability Insurance program (OASDI) – is not a tax per se. It is a deduction from money that *we earn,* which goes to a fund (the Social Security Trust Fund) to protect our loved ones and us when we age, die or become disabled. So-called "tax" collectors may collect it, but it is not a tax. The Bush Administration's drive to push roughly one-third of our mandatory Social Security contribution into private accounts sounds like a great idea until you consider its practical reality.

First of all, President Bush's proposed program is hardly "private." Unless you are adept at investing, your choices will be limited. Essentially you and your fellow Americans will likely be driving in separate vehicles, of varying horsepower, without a map, and be subject to "accidents" and "hijackings" along the "Wall Street highway." Secondly, it is not a "small amount." Although the White House is talking about starting with a third of payroll deductions (roughly 4% of our gross wages), this is a classic case of "give 'em and inch and they'll take a mile." Mark my words: an out-of-touch Congress will ratchet up that 4% diversion of our gross wages until the Fund is devoid of participants and people are at the mercy of the stock market. Does anyone remember the "Black Friday" market crashes of 1929, 1987, and 2000?

There is, however, a simple and relatively clean solution. If Bush and the Republican-dominated Congress want people to have more for retirement, why not simply create a universal, tax-exempt, investment program that is an adjunct to the Social Security Fund program? They will not take this path because they do not want to be responsible for keeping the Fund's promises. Depending on whom you talk to, the Fund will not experience a shortfall until 2042 or 2052 but no one in Congress knows for sure. Even then it will be able to pay 80% of what someone expects to receive. How much more would need to be deducted from our payrolls to cover that shortfall? There is a two-part answer to this question:

The first part has to do with the power of compound interest – the sooner we start an ancillary savings program, the sooner we will have built up a fund base large enough to cover any shortfall;

The second part is that the percentage increase in payroll deduction required needs to be determined honestly and without partisanship. The only way we will know, the only way to achieve that answer, is to get rid of any Congressman or woman who cannot tell us. In other words, elect the kind of ombudsmen that are envisioned by The DayLight Movement. In other words, elect wisdom.

"The true danger is when liberty is nibbled away, for expedience, and by parts." *Edmund Burke*

The same can be said for our cash. George W. Bush's handlers are betting that you'll buy their fear mongering and permit them to push you, alone, onto Wall Street. Today it's just a portion of our old age, survivor and disability fund money. Sooner than later, a year from now, five years from now or ten, it'll be *all* of our Social Security money sucked into what has been termed "the greatest casino on earth." In his quest to be defined for posterity, President Bush has once again proven that not only can he not get the solution right he cannot even get the problem right. The plain truth is that Social Security is OK, and, with minor modification, will continue to be OK – that is, if we can keep Congress' hands off of the Fund.

Any parent knows that letting children make their own decisions sounds good in theory, but in reality there are times when we absolutely must step in and make a decision for them; it is called "parental responsibility." In the healthiest of parent-child relationships, when the kids get older and move away, their parents let them know that they are on their own; but if they screw up, Mom & Dad are always there to help. That is the essence of Social Security: if you are short of money upon disability or retirement, or your passing leaves your family financially bereft, there will be a modest "social safety net" to help.

In an ideal world, everyone would have the time, health, wisdom, and income to plan for unforeseen events and to invest wisely for retirement. There would be no insider trading or con men lurking on Wall Street; there would be no oil company executives raiding their company treasury while advising the Vice President in secret energy policy meetings and exhorting their employees and the public to buy company stock as they sell their own; there would be no "Internet bubble" market hysteria skewing the market upward and then suddenly taking the entire thing down, including non-Internet stocks. But we know that is not the way life works. A majority of Americans putting a significant amount of their "absolutely-have-to-have-this-money-when-I-retire-or-die" funds into such a "casino" environment is a recipe for a national financial disaster that would make the Great Depression look like a rounding error in our national checkbook.

If you want to know who controls George W. Bush, just stop and think: even a moron (and he is no moron) knows that, if you want to invest efficiently, en masse, in the private equity markets, you do it by letting the government invest on a united, high-volume, basis rather than by forcing individuals to fend for themselves and pay heavy commissions and fees. Why do we have to invest this "privatized" money ourselves? Why doesn't our government do it for us? Answer: Because if a special government manager does the investing, the only ones who get cut out will be Bush's and Congress' Wall Street fee and commission-driven financial patrons.

But, before we go down this particular path, jointly or severally, we need to ask, "what effect, if any, would such a massive long-term investment have on our, and perhaps the world's stock markets?" Has anyone figured out how much illiquid capital our financial markets can absorb? After all, this money is not going to be placed short term. One can liken it to the question of how much rain a hillside can absorb before a mudslide occurs. Will investments be made simply for investment's (i.e., "parking" money's") sake? Will fund managers get sloppy? On the flip side, a potential benefit may be that, knowing that this money is in for the long-term, corporate CEOs may not feel as much pressure to manage for short-term, quarterly, results.

This is irreplaceable long-term retirement money we are talking about. Even if there was a single-source, government-managed, master investment program, do we really want to put our retirement money into a market that, in the throes of the Internet hysteria period, valued *start-ups* at as much as 1,000 times *projected* earnings? To hope that "the next new thing" might come along to bail out our economy is tantamount to providing for your children's education and your retirement by purchasing lottery tickets.
We-the-People would have to ensure that there is a well-thought-out "prudent man" rule governing such an all-inclusive master program. What about liquidity for individuals, and market volatility? What happens when a large

class of retirees, like the current "Baby Boomer" population, wants to unload their investment positions at virtually the same time? Can you imagine the feeding frenzy of short-selling sharks that would be awaiting them?

Just as providing quality healthcare to ensure a physically healthy populace is important to our national fitness, a social safety net under our oldest and most vulnerable fellow citizens is equally important – at least until we find a way to create a democracy that is characterized not by its financial wealth but rather by how the least of its members live. I am not talking about communism; I am talking about taking care of each other and our selves in a fiscally responsible manner.

In our headlong rush through a materialistic 20th century, we lost track of the fact that we all are part of a larger national organism. If one of us is ill or poor, all of us, to some degree are ill or poor. You may not write a check to a poor person directly, but you're paying into social programs in one form or another and paying higher hospital bills to offset those who are indigent and cannot pay to stay alive. Only when we return to a caring national culture with a level playing field of laws and opportunity can we start talking about taking personal responsibility for ourselves and no one else. But, ironically, at that point we likely will not want to think that way.

There would not be a Social Security Fund shortfall if Congress would stop treating it like a piggy bank whenever it runs a healthy surplus. The same could be said for the managers of private corporate pension plans who have ruined countless lives and plans for the sunset years of people who played the game fair-and-square, only to be cheated out of what they had been promised. If any of our so-called "We-know-what's-good-for-you-better-than-you-do" experts try to tell you that the retiree's plight is simply a result of failing to read the *fine print* on their company's pension plan, they are lying. Many plans never had any provision for the "legal looting" or corporate bankruptcies that took place. Even if they did, who wants to live in a society and work for companies where small print determines our fate? How much would you be willing to bet that the senior executives of these kinds of companies ensured that *their* contracts contained no such "fine print?" Just as corporate pension scofflaws do, Bush & Co.'s push to privatize Social Security is nothing more than a ploy to dump a problem onto the very people who will be hurt the most, and to enrich Bush's Big Money handlers while they are at it.

Social Security was never supposed to be anyone's sole source of retirement income. The average interest yield on our contributions to the Fund is modest but more secure than millions of us – some well informed and others not – are likely to achieve by trying to pick investments in individual stocks, bonds or even mutual funds. The thinking behind this "forced savings" Social Security program reflects the fact that most human beings do not have the discipline to actually save. In fact, compared to the rest of the civilized world, we have one of the lowest personal savings rates. Thus, the payroll deduction protocol was a good way to ensure that at least some money for our sunset years actually survived our consumption-obsessed, "got-to-have-it-now" society and made it into a secure account.

Bush and his Wall Street buddies want us to believe that we can change our spots and become savers. What is he basing this on? While government should be as non-intrusive and benign as possible, there are times when, like that previously mentioned proverbial parent, it must step in and take action for our own good. That is why we need to quickly design and implement a *mandatory* savings program that is connected to the current Social Security net and, if it must be largely self-guided, then within certain mandated parameters to ensure that something is available when it is time to cash out. The current $700 Billion Medicare Prescription debacle is reason enough to get the Social Security challenge behind us so we can concentrate on this even larger looming disaster.

Amassing proceeds to pay the cost of a truly reliable personal/governmental social safety net must begin early in a person's life. It is likely too late for most of the present adult generation but, for those under 40, it is better late than never. To those who say that more government involvement will move us toward a socialistic system like Sweden and Denmark, I say we are doing it anyway. Instead of just taxing the daylights out of people so we can pay for things like Medicare, we do it via a circuitous route: we *borrow* huge sums of money to fund programs like Medicare and then saddle our children and grandchildren with an enormous obligation to repay that debt.

The damage to our economy that has been perpetrated by decades of inept Congresses can be likened to rust: you can stop it but you cannot reverse it. We need to muster the courage to increase individual savings and to stop borrowing money, both individually and as a nation. As described in the previous chapter, a simple head tax and a balanced budget will provide us with extra money to save and, eventually, put America back on a sound financial footing.

Don't think that the Bush team has given up on privatizing Social Security. When faced with public resistance, they just back off for a while as if we were children who will soon forget about whatever was bothering us. Like he did with his original rationale for invading Iraq, President Bush now parrots another "lie of fear" fed to him by his handlers – a lie intended to panic and herd us into their financial slaughterhouse. They are relying on us to buy into the logic that investment in the stock market will yield a much higher return than that currently achieved through the Social Security Fund. But, if their privatization model had been in place when the Internet bubble burst, the stock market cratered, and you had retired just a month too late, your "privatized nest egg" would have been *half* that of someone who retired at the peak of that insane market run-up.

150 MILLION ACCOUNTS: LIKE HERDING CATS

In Dr. Barry Schwartz' seminal Op-Ed piece, "Choose and Lose," published in *The New York Times* on January 5, 2005, he quoted Dean Baker, co-director of the Center for Economic Policy Research, as saying that, "the administrative costs of keeping track of these private accounts... will be 10 to 30 times the cost of administering the current system, eating up almost all of the hypothetical gains that equity investments could provide." Now, if Dr. Schwartz knows this and the readership of *The New York Times* now know this, why don't Bush and his top advisors know this? With all due respect for their intellect, the Social Security issue is complex. As vociferous a cheerleader as he has been, does anyone really think that the president has suddenly become sufficiently educated to realize what he is so ardently advocating? Have he and his handlers considered the costs of administering and monitoring 150 million disparate investment accounts? Have they even considered the fact that, as was eloquently put by Dr. Schwarz, "... the diversion of money into individual accounts would save the government nothing, since it would have to borrow to offset the loss of the diverted dollars'? 'The individual accounts represent a transfer, not a savings.'"

Bush sycophant and fellow crisis-mongerer, Stephen Moore, author of *''Bullish on Bush: How George W. Bush's Ownership Society Will Make America Stronger,''* asserts that ''we call it [privatization of Social Security] a conservative New Deal. It will be a fundamental shift from an entitlement society to an ownership society.'' In their blind rush to support yet another destructive attack on our constitutional rights, Mr. Moore and our President conveniently overlook the fact that, unlike straight welfare, we already own the money in the Social Security Fund. It is *our* money; we *earned* it. Their mindset seems clear: "whenever you can't keep your promises, just change them or change the game." With our administration holding this kind of attitude, it is clear that we must either clean up our national culture or watch America go the way of every once-dominant-turned-decadent society since the beginning of time.

> **"All that is necessary for evil to triumph is for good men to do nothing."**
> *Edmund Burke*

One thing that can help the Social Security Fund remain healthy is to institute fairness on a higher plane. Because its true nature is that of a safety net, not a savings account, people who were fortunate or industrious enough to end up with a high level of income and assets should not draw down on the Social Security Fund. A large reason why anyone succeeds in America (or any country, for that matter) is not simply due solely to his or her unilateral efforts. They need others to work for them and with them and to buy from or sell to them. They need others to fight fires, to repair the streets and to build the vehicles that take them to the place where they earn their living. Whether we want to admit it or not, we are all in this together. Those who were more fortunate in life need to act with generosity and nobility toward those less fortunate.

Privatizing Social Security, or even the more workable concept of letting the government privately invest some of our Fund money, may be a solution that is coming too late in light of the ascendancy of competitors for economic superpower status, like the European Union and China. Their rise will certainly impact our equity and debt markets and, in turn, affect the quality of financial returns that can be achieved from private or even quasi-private accounts. What frightens me the most about Bush's ill-conceived privatization gambit is that it will likely prove impossible to pass the House, so Bush's minions will settle for a half-baked face-saving measure that may actually be worse than what they are proposing now.

If the current Congress will do the right thing by Social Security i.e. raise the payroll tax, eliminate the $90,000 limit on wages taxed for Social Security (those at this level can afford it), raise the eligibility age to 70 (thanks to an abysmally low personal savings rate, most of us will have to work that long anyway), increase the current Social Security "tax" from 15.3 to 18 percent (this assumes that we do not adopt a simple head tax), exclude those with a to-be-determined-but-fair high net worth, and mandate separate minimum savings accounts, then we can forgive the failure of all the previous Congresses that raided and abused the Fund. This is a classic example of the value of our DayLight process. We-the-People will bypass flinching politicians who are afraid to make decisions that will not get them reelected. Instead, we will face up to hard decisions without trying to hide behind complexity and the window-dressing intended to make those decisions look more appealing.

CHAPTER 7

PENSIONS

The backpedaling and rationalizing that is going on in America's pension system is a classic example of why we need to bring a new, ombudsman-type leadership into every level of elective office. A front-page article titled, "Major Changes Raise Concerns on Pension Bill" *(The New York Times, March 19, 2006)* reported that,

> "Congress set out more than a year ago to fashion legislation that would protect America's private pension system ... Then the political horse-trading began, with lawmakers, companies and lobbyists, representing everything from big Wall Street firms to tiny rural electric cooperatives, weighing in on the particulars of the Bush administration's blueprint.
>
> In the end, lawmakers modified many of the proposed rules, allowing companies more time to cover pension shortfalls, to make more forgiving estimates about how much they will owe workers in the future, and even sometimes to assume that their workers will die younger than the rest of the population.
>
> On top of those changes, companies also persuaded lawmakers to add dozens of specific measures, including a multibillion-dollar escape clause for the nation's airlines and a special exemption for the makers of Smithfield Farms hams.
>
> As a result, the bill now being completed in a House-Senate conference committee, rather than strengthening the pension system, would actually weaken it, according to a little-noticed analysis by the government's pension agency....That shortfall raises the specter of more pension plans failing, pushing their liabilities on to the government."

What a joke it was to hear our elected leaders suddenly decrying all of the pension system abuse and loopholes after committing benign neglect for decades until their misdeeds were shoved right under their noses and they were forced to acknowledge them. Credit the press for blowing this whistle. In the October 30, 2005 issue of *The New York Times*, Roger Lowenstein writes: "A pension plan can afford to support people who live to be 90 because some of its members will expire at 66. This is why a 401(k) is not a true substitute." The same can be said about Social Security vs. private social security plans.

Another *New York Times* article, "Whoops! There Goes Another Pension Plan" (September 17, 2005), describes a common tactic:

> "Robert S. Miller is a turnaround artist with a Dickensian twist. He unlocks hidden value in floundering Rust Belt companies by jettisoning their pension plans. His approach, copied by executives at airlines and other troubled companies, can make the people who rely on his very rich. But it may be creating a multibillion-dollar mess for taxpayers later.
>
> As chief executive of Bethlehem Steel in 2002, Mr. Miller shut down the pension plan, leaving a federal program to meet the company's $3.7 billion in unfunded obligations to retirees. That turned the moribund company into a prime acquisition target. Wilbur L. Ross, a so-called vulture investor, snapped it up, combined it with four other dying steel makers he bought at about the same time, and sold the resulting company for $4.5 Billion – a return of more than 1,000 percent in just three years on the $400 million he paid for all five companies."

Once again, the root solution to these immoral travesties is a relatively simple one: corporate pension plans must meet the same regulatory standards as life insurance companies. An issuing corporation must maintain adequate reserves to cover all claims and must not change their plan's terms and conditions. Can you imagine buying life insurance only to have the issuer tell your heirs that, due to miscalculation and mismanagement (if not outright criminal acts of fraud and looting), they will not be getting a penny? How could so many Congresses have let this disaster-in-the-making continue for decades? What does it say about our national culture and values if, somehow, it is OK to renege on pension promises to citizens who have worked hard their whole lives? If ever there was an example of why we need to change our current system of government – and why we need the DayLight Movement – here it is.

There also is a movement afoot in Congress to repeal a pension law that "...bars companies with richly financed pension plans from taking any of the surplus money out, except in rare instances." This law has been mightily abused by corporate leaders focused on the short-term bottom line rather than on their pension fund's intended purpose of taking care of those who make that bottom line possible.

When will our business and political leaders admit to the fact that, in the cyclical business world, there is no such thing as a "surplus" that can be tapped at any time? In the 1980s, some of the companies that pulled out enormous amounts of pension money for things like corporate reorganizations and leveraged acquisitions turn up today as having the nation's most under-funded pension plans. United Airlines raided $254 million out of its employee's pension fund in 1985, and now it says it cannot keep its pension plans going any longer and expects them to be taken over by the federal pension insurance agency. Would that be the case today if United had kept its hands off those funds and allowed the magic of compound interest to do its thing? Why aren't the executives, who approved this outright theft (and the Congressional law makers who permitted it), behind bars?

In that same March 19, 2006 article, *The New York Times* reports that, "The bills would also be a boon to Wall Street by permitting financial service companies to handle more retirement money with fewer restrictions. Hedge funds, for example, would be permitted to manage more pension money without being held to the pension law's exacting standards of fiduciary duty." In the August 20, 2005 issue of *The New York Times*, the newspaper's "What's Offline" column put forth a most sobering thought: "For those who worry about the solvency of your pension funds, here is more fuel for the fire. Some 23 percent of pension managers surveyed by *Alpha magazine* say they currently invest in hedge funds – private, unregulated investments." All of these practices beg the question of how Americans can save money for their hard-earned retirement when their elected politicians are recklessly extracting it from them by inappropriate spending and lax investor protection and pension laws.

We-the-People need to get rid of the varying definitions of what a pension plan is, and how it can be manipulated. There should be a single, simple rule: **if you hire someone and promise them a pension in addition to salary, then that money is locked in and cannot be taken out until the person retires or leaves the company; and when they do leave, they should be able to transfer their pension dollars to their new employer's fund.**

We need to put people, who neglect or otherwise fool with our pensions, in jail and not for just a "wrist slap" of a sentence. It will be interesting to see how companies that choose not to protect their pension programs can attract great employees when they must fully disclose the fact that the light at the end of their working-years tunnel is really the headlamp of an oncoming locomotive.

One final point: There is a growing movement afoot by corporate employers to eliminate pension plans. This may look good on an Excel spreadsheet but, unless they are willing to pay employees enough to permit them to save money for retirement, how will this make any difference in the long run from a financial perspective or from an international competition perspective? One of the driving factors in favor of pension plan contributions was our archaic tax code. A simple sales or head tax system (or a combination) would permit a clearer path from a worker to his or her money. Then we could really roll up our sleeves and work on realistic solutions to our nation's social security.

CHAPTER 8

WELFARE

"How can there possibly be liberty and justice for all, when, in the name of justice, people claim rights to income, food, housing, education, health care, transportation, ad infinitum? We can't. Positive rights to receive such things, absent an obligation to earn them, must violate others' liberty, by taking some of their income without their consent. They are really just wishes, convertible into benefits for some only by employing the government to violate others' rights not to have what is theirs taken."
Pepperdine Professor Gary Galles, 2004

WELFARE = WORKFARE.

I am a strong believer in "Whatever happens to the least of us happens to all of us." Why do you think that crime increases in direct proportion to our nation's current state of affairs at any given point in time? A prime example is the looting that we see after natural disasters. Such acts tell us that people commit monetary-oriented crimes more out of desperation than because they are evil. We do our society and our selves a favor by eliminating as much of that desperation as possible but without weakening the recipient of our aid by taking away their incentive to work.

Welfare is a "safety net" intended only to catch someone from freefalling, not hold him or her in a lifelong relaxation hammock. Begun as something that was supposed to help people for a short time, our public welfare system quickly grew into something akin to slavery; resulting in a loss of initiative and self-esteem that traps blacks and whites alike and destroys the traditional family structure of virtually all who it is supposed to benefit.

As a consequence, the male authority figure largely disappeared from the welfare family and so did his influence; especially on his male children who grew up emulating his emasculated visage and feeling of hopelessness. How do you expect a man to work when he can take home more from welfare than he can from gainful employment? How is he to maintain his status as provider and head-of-household?

We will tap the collective intelligence of our fellow DayLight members for the purpose of finding a way to ensure that the greatest nation in the world has a bottom rung on its socioeconomic ladder from which the least of us can begin to climb out of whatever financial or emotional "sand hole" they may be in. Instead of spending billions of dollars and thousands of American lives on war and "foreign nation building," we will take care of those who cannot take care of themselves or who simply need a boost onto that proverbial ladder's first rung. That will be the mark of a truly great nation.

While it would be premature to suggest whether the following idea is a good one or not, it represents the kind of "thinking outside the box" that will be needed to solve the challenges of the poor: Using the DayLight Forum as a place to recruit people with wisdom and experience, perhaps one of the many things that we could explore is to take a lesson from the aftermath of hurricane's Katrina and Rita. If hundreds of thousands of evacuees could be moved to safety and permanent residence under such urgent and trying circumstances, why couldn't we create an opportunity to assist ten times that number of unemployed people to move in an orderly and dignified manner to parts of the country where they can find employment?

A comment from the April 22, 2006 edition of *The New York Times* ("Katrina's Tide Carries Many to Hopeful Shores") seems to reinforce this suggestion: "... one surprising benefit from an otherwise terrible storm: the exodus took low-income families to areas richer in opportunity. *The New York Times* analyzed relocation patterns in 17 counties in and around Atlanta and Houston, two leading destinations for Katrina evacuees ... the average evacuee has landed in a neighborhood with nearly twice the income as the one left behind, less than half as much poverty, and significantly higher levels of education, employment and home ownership."

Sometimes people just need to know that help to make such a move is available. Whether further exploration determines this to be a good or bad idea is not as important as the fact that we will be "thinking outside the box" (and the Beltway) to solve what has been, to-date, unsolvable.

INTERNATIONAL WELFARE

Anyone with a television set has likely seen heartrending pleas for donations to feed, clothe and house desperately poor adults and children in other countries. I confess that I have contributed to a number of them and continue to do so, but these pitches have been going on for decades. Have our contributions worked? Are we really doing the recipients any good or are we acting in a co-dependent manner, enabling them to remain weak and needy generation after generation? Do we help their perpetual situation by *giving* food, clothing and housing that they do not have to earn? Those of us who contribute have to work for the money that we give. The Bible tells us to feed and clothe the poor but it does not say anything about them not earning our help fair and square. One of the many topics to be debated and decided at the DayLight Forum will be, "Should the world apply 'tough love' and let a single generation of a perpetually needy nation die in order to teach these recipients a lesson that, in the long run, will save countless future generations? How far do we go to save people from themselves? Do we let them know that there will be no aid without mandatory education, possible relocation, work, and serious birth control – perhaps even sterilization?" This discussion cannot begin soon enough.

Give a man a fish, and you feed him for a day; teach him how to catch fish, and you feed him for a lifetime. *(Chinese proverb)*

CHAPTER 9

IMMIGRATION

"Until now, the focus has been on the 10 million or so illegal aliens to whom the bill would give amnesty. But the bill would admit far more immigrants: 103 million---or one-third the current U.S. population---over the next 20 years." *The Heritage Foundation*

I fear that, by the time this book is published, our conflicted Congress may have made a terrible mistake that will have dire and unnecessary financial ramifications for all of us.

In late 2004 the state of New York proposed that non-U.S. citizens be given the right to vote (a politically motivated welfare virus that would spread across the country as *they* spread across the country). We will do our elected officials a favor by relieving them of decisions about giving illegal aliens the right to vote them into power. As bad as things are, we haven't seen many Special Interest "monsters" with this much negative potential.

Why is it that anytime someone decries the invasion of our country by people who do not respect our laws enough to enter legally they are accused of racism, fear, and repression? While I do not doubt her sincerity, Senator Hillary Clinton denounced the current immigration crackdown ("Mrs. Clinton Says G.O.P.'s Immigration Plan Is at Odds With the Bible" *The New York Times*, March 23, 2006) asserting, "It is certainly not in keeping with my understanding of the Scripture because this bill would literally criminalize the Good Samaritan and probably even Jesus himself," she said. Someone should remind the good senator that Jesus also advised us to obey just laws.

What is unjust about preventing people from taking, without permission, what belongs to us? She went on to say that, "We need to sound the alarm about what is being done in the Congress." We also need to sound the alarm about a criminal invasion that is sucking our tax dollars out of an already mis-managed state and federal budget system and raising genuine concern about who among these trespassers is also a terrorist (while the focus is on our border with Mexico, in good faith I should mention that there has been considerable conjecture that the 19 hijackers of 9/11 entered our country via Canada).

Congress and law enforcement (excuse the oxymoron) have permitted this illegal invasion go on for so long and in such overwhelming numbers that now, in their inane wisdom, our elected officials have "thrown up their hands" and are allowing themselves to be pressured into blessing these invaders and their unbelievably nervy protest marches.

For proof that illegal immigrants are already present and *united* in alarming numbers, one need look no farther than the hundreds of thousands of "immigrant rights" protesters who, in the spring of 2006, marched in the cities where they are prevalent. These parades consisted largely of illegal aliens and school kids who do not yet know how difficult it is to support a family without also having to pay a hefty tab for illegal entrants who drain our healthcare and school systems.

The American public has eyes and is too intelligent to miss the farce in these marches. What do you think would happen if the nation's home invasion robbers staged a protest march? Can you imagine the crackdown that would come down upon their heads? Why the difference? They're both invaders. The difference is, burglars don't have a constituency of sympathetic-but-misguided naturalized citizens who came before these immigration outlaws and are now trying to vote them in. Once you let the camel's nose under the side of your tent....

Our failure to enforce our laws has bred an insidious "societal cancer" that, based on their numbers and lawbreaking longevity, is now vociferously demanding Constitutional protection. Self-righteous protesters are pressuring our elected officials – many of whom are afraid of losing the vote of sympathetic-but-misguided naturalized citizens who came before these outlaws – to further weaken our immigration policy. If we do not stop them now, we may never be able to. All these illegals have to do is come in under the law, learn to speak English, get a job (any job), obey our laws, and I will gladly fight for their rights to fair and humane treatment. Otherwise, while the treatment they receive may indeed be harsh, it is likely a useful, and perhaps the only effective, deterrent.

Although it is impossible to say precisely how many illegal immigrants reside in the United States, because they are not going to readily identify themselves, a January 3, 2005 report entitled *"The Underground Labor Force*

Is Rising To The Surface," by Robert Justich and Betty Ng, CFA at Wall Street investment bank Bear Stearns, estimated that:

> "The number of illegal immigrants in the United States may be as high as 20 million people, more than double the official 9 million people estimated by the Census Bureau. The total number of legalized immigrants entering the United States since 1990 has averaged 962,000 per year. Several credible studies indicate that the number of illegal entries has recently crept up to 30 million per year, triple the authorized figure, and that undocumented immigrants are gaining a larger share of the job market, and hold approximately 12 to 15 million jobs in the United States (8% of the employed)."

Illegal aliens now comprise 6% of our total population. That is three times the total Jewish population, eight times more than there are American Indians, and roughly half as many as there are African-Americans. The fact that most of our country's corporate and governmental interactive voice response telephone systems now offer a choice between English and Spanish is stark confirmation of many Americans' feeling of being overrun by illegal entrants who primarily invade California and Arizona, by the thousands, day and night, 365 days a year.

Immigration is one issue where the good intentions of the "bleeding heart" segment of the liberal movement have really hurt us as a nation, and yet we continue to permit this socioeconomic "parasite" to invade our homeland. Illegal immigrants have successfully established a beachhead from which more of their kind can slip in, and we are rapidly approaching a saturation point where "have-nots" who could not make it in their own country suck up welfare and healthcare dollars, overburden our schools, and may soon be able to vote our country into bankruptcy.

The special interest clout of the immigrant community is growing with each passing day. A vicious societal cycle is already in full swing: a cycle that has trapped our politicians in a "black hole" that threatens to pull the rest of us in with them. By not getting tough on immigration and by enacting overly generous legislation and societal programs that are like "honey to bees," our elected officials have fostered an invasion of largely unskilled "have-nots" who expect to be treated as our equals.

Once these individuals get in, they have children who are born into citizenship and who grow up to vote for politicians who will allow more of their foreign relatives to invade our land and siphon off our hard-earned national wealth.

We-the-People cannot afford to have our right to vote given away to those who refuse to play by the rules and obey the laws that any stable society must maintain. If we do not take a firm stand now, they will become the majority and vote us out of house and home. We must stop this shredding of our country's basic fabric while America is still recognizable. We need to restore dignity to our right to vote – a right that should not be for sale by politicians in their never-ending quest for votes and cash.

A classic case-in-point was made by an article in the *Washington Post* ("Immigration Issue Threatens GOP's Fla. Stronghold – Cuban Americans Angry Over 'Wet Foot' Policy," February 17, 2006), which described a political furor in Florida by Cuban Americans who were protesting what is known as a "wet foot, dry foot" policy that allows Cubans fleeing communism to reside in the United States if they reach dry land. While most Cuban immigrants have distinguished themselves as hardworking, productive, U.S. citizens, it is still troubling to think that, because we humanely relaxed our immigration policy for this special group (favoring them over others who were equally deserving), they are now here in such electoral numbers as to be able to force politicians to bend the rules even further; thereby adding to their ranks and further transforming south Florida into a virtual south American nation. Bend anything far enough and frequently enough and eventually it will break.

NOT AN OPEN CHECKBOOK

When, in the name of political expediency, we permit illegal aliens to leapfrog both our immigration laws and the people who apply legally, we are letting in a distorted mindset of entitlement and poor values that is toxic to our culture. It is time that We-the-People send a message back across our borders that our laws must be taken seriously and will be enforced. We need to stop taking in immigrants, especially unskilled minorities, until we can care for, respect and absorb the ones that we already have. But, first, we must take care of *our own* needy citizens before we pile more onto an already overloaded system. This has never been more salient than in the aftermath of Hurricane Katrina, when we saw true pain and suffering on the faces of our own people, in our own land. This is not being xenophobic; it is common sense, and far more humane than continuing to compound the problem that improperly managed immigration brings.

As the old adage goes, "The Lord helps those who help themselves." If people are unhappy with the way things are in their homeland, then, instead of fleeing, they must unite to effect change and, if need be, to spill their own blood on their own soil. It is time we send a message to other countries that, although we care about our fellow human beings, they must clean up their own messes, not export them here in an endless wave of unskilled, sometimes criminal, asylum seekers – legal or illegal. Our welfare system simply cannot bear much more of it. We-the-People want to help, but our nation is not an open checkbook meant to ease the woes of the world. It does us no good to act as such, and, in the long run, it does the oppressed peoples of the world no good either; in fact, it perpetuates their weakness. The solution is not to run away from their problems; the solution is to face them.

BAD MANNERED GUESTS

We seem to have forgotten that, originally, we opened America's door to our fellow men from foreign lands in the same spirit that we would invite someone into our home. As a guest in someone's home, you do not suddenly demand that your host change his or her values and way of life. You do not speak in an unintelligible language or converse openly just amongst your fellow foreign guests in the presence of your host or employer. Egged on by the well-meaning American Civil Liberties Union (ACLU), new immigrants have subverted a basic behavioral ground rule: "When in Rome, do as the Romans do."

Our country was founded on a belief in God. For most of us that means "Christianity." For those of other faiths who would have been excluded from many countries, to come in and start making waves in our societal "living room" is more than bad form; it is hostile and threatening to the nature and quality of American life. If you wish to practice special cultural or religious beliefs, we will support you as long as you do it on your own time in your own place. Don't try to change the game after we let you in and, in this age of terror, don't be so ridiculously obtuse as to insist on wearing a veil for your driver's license photo.

Lately the terms "immigration" and "illegal alien" have become almost automatically equated with being "Mexican." While Hispanics have been in the public eye via their highly publicized marches, the truth is that illegal aliens come from all 4 corners of the world. Having said that, I offer a "real world" perspective on the Hispanic influx from someone who deals with illegal immigrants on a daily basis. The following letter from a retired teacher has been passed around on the Internet and has made it to my e-mail box on more than one occasion. While this one is from California, friends in Texas have reported the same vexing environment. Clearly our pontificating politicians are clueless about what is really going on and whom they think they are letting in:

From a retired teacher friend whose wife still teaches in the Riverside, California area:

"As you all listen to the news about the student protests over illegal immigration there are some things that you should be aware of. As most of you know my wife is in charge of the English-as-a-second-language department at large southern California high school, which is designated a Title 1 school, meaning that its students average lower socio-economic and income levels. Most of the schools you are hearing about –South Gate High, Bell Gardens, Huntington Park, CA., etc. – where these students are protesting, are also Title 1 schools. My wife tells me that 100% of the students in her school and other Title 1 schools are on the free breakfast, free lunch program. When I say free breakfast I'm not talking a glass of milk and roll...but a full breakfast and cereal bar with fruits and juices that would make a Marriott proud. The waste of this food is monumental, with trays and trays of it being dumped in the trash uneaten. She estimates that well over 50% of these students are obese or at least moderately overweight. About 75% or more DO have cell phones. The school also provides day-care centers for the unwed teenage pregnant girls (some as young as 13) so they can attend class without the inconvenience of having to arrange for baby-sitters or having family watch their kids. My wife was ordered to spend $700,000 on her department or risk losing funding for the upcoming year even though there was little need for anything; her budget was already substantial. She ended up buying new computers for their computer-learning center; half of which, one month later, have been carved with graffiti by the 'appreciative students who obviously feel humbled and grateful to have a free education in America.' She has had to intervene several times for young and substitute teachers whose classes consist of many illegal immigrant students here in the country less then 3 months who raised so much hell with the female teachers, calling them "Putas" (whores) and throwing things that the teachers were in tears Free medical, free education, free food, day care etc., etc., etc, Is it any wonder they feel entitled to not only be in this country but to demand rights, privileges and entitlement? I hope you realize that the last 3 presidents have allowed this to come to this horrendous state of affairs. It didn't happen overnight. To my friends who want to point out how much these illegal immigrants contribute to our society because they LIKE their gardener and housekeeper and they like to pay less for tomatoes: spend some time in the real world of illegal immigration and see the TRUE costs. Higher insurance, a LOT more crime, CLOSING Medical facilities, higher medical costs, lower standards of education in our schools, overcrowding, new diseases etc., etc., etc. We are being overtaxed to pay for their free EVERYTHING. I'd rather pay more for tomatoes! We need to wake up. The guest worker program will be a disaster because we won't have the guts to enforce it. Does anyone in their right mind really think they will leave and return voluntarily? There are many hardworking Hispanic/American citizens that contribute to our country and many that I consider my true friends. We all encourage and accept those Hispanics who have done it the right and legal way. They are very welcome in the U.S. It does, however, have everything to do with culture: A third-world culture that does not value education, that accepts children getting pregnant and dropping out of school by 15 and that refuses to assimilate...and an American culture that has become so weak and politically correct that we don't have the will to do anything about it. If this makes your blood boil, as it did mine, forward this to everyone you know."

An article from *The New York Times* ("Maine: Limit To Questions On Citizenship," April 13, 2004) illuminates just how low and ridiculously illogical some vote-pandering, cynically "politically correct" politicians will stoop:

"Gov. John Baldacci has signed an executive order limiting the circumstances in which state employees can ask about the immigration status of residents seeking services. The order allows employees to ask about the status only in specific situations: when such disclosure is required by law, for example, or when the resident is suspected of unlawful activity other than being in the country illegally. Mr. Baldacci, a Democrat, signed the order after meetings with social service, civil rights, and community organizations. The sessions were held to help ease relations between the groups and state officials after Border Patrol agents swept through stores, restaurants, and a homeless shelter in Portland in January."

Isn't that what our Border Patrol and other immigration law enforcement personnel are *supposed* to do? Why should we limit our right to protect ourselves? And speaking of our Border Patrol, here is an excerpt of a letter that was sent to Senator William Frist by David J. Stoddard U.S. Border Patrol (RET) Hereford, Arizona:

"Dear Senator Frist:
There is a huge amount of propaganda and myths circulating about illegal aliens, particularly illegal Mexican, Salvadorian, Guatemalan and Honduran aliens.

Illegal aliens generally do NOT want U.S. citizenship. Americans are very vain thinking that everybody in the world wants to be a U.S. citizen. Mexicans, and other nationalities want to remain citizens of their home countries while obtaining the benefits offered by the United States such as employment, medical care, in-state tuition, government subsidized housing and free education for their offspring. Their main attraction is employment and their loyalty usually remains at home. They want benefits earned and subsidized by middle class Americans. What illegal aliens want are benefits of American residence without paying the price. ... Every person who illegally entered this nation left a home. They are NOT homeless and they are NOT Americans. Some left jobs in their home countries. They come to send money to their real home as evidenced by the more than 20 billion dollars sent out of the country each year by illegal aliens. These illegal aliens knowingly and willfully entered this nation in violation of the law and therefore assumed the risk of detection and deportation. Those who brought their alien children assumed the responsibility and risk on behalf of their children ...Illegal aliens are NOT critical to

> the economy. Illegal aliens constitute less than 5% of the workforce. However, they reduce wages and benefits for lawful U.S. residents."

With regard to the above-referenced $20 Billion (some say $30 Billion) of untaxed dollars that these scofflaws send home annually, "Friend of Day-Light," Michael Frank, suggests that we tax all dollars wired or otherwise conveyed out of the country unless the sender can prove that he or she paid income tax on that money. The $5-10 Billion of tax revenue derived from this policy could help defray some of the expense associated with protecting our borders and help a hospital system that is being bankrupted by illegal aliens who use our emergency rooms as health clinics.

A DISHONEST AND SELF-SERVING ECONOMIC RATIONALE

Granting amnesty to illegal aliens because our economy needs them is a specious argument that benefits no one except those who are taking advantage of a covert, cheap labor force. America is a country based on capitalism and the law of supply and demand. If this illegal workforce were not here, the people now employing them would be forced to pay market rates and employ real Americans who are currently unemployed and waiting for an opportunity to contribute to, rather than take from, our economy.

In the February 12th edition of the Internet newsletter *CounterPunch* (www.counterpunch.org) Paul Craig Roberts, Assistant Secretary of the Treasury in the Reagan administration, former Associate Editor of the Wall Street Journal editorial page and Contributing Editor of National Review writes:

> "Forget Iran, Americans Should be Hysterical About This: Job growth over the last five years is the weakest on record. The U.S. economy came up more than 7 million jobs short of keeping up with population growth. That's one good reason for controlling immigration. An economy that cannot keep up with population growth should not be boosting population with heavy rates of legal and illegal immigration."

ILLEGAL?
NO DRIVER'S LICENSE, NO WELFARE, NO RIGHTS.

As for those immigrants who do not work, it is important to remember that welfare is for hardworking citizens with a *temporary* problem; it is not a right and tool of immigration. Misguided "bleeding-heart" protection of "have-nots" who will not work threatens to overwhelm our country with a welfare electoral majority that will suck the life out of our finances and the financial future of our children. We need to institute a rule that no immigrant is eligible until they have been naturalized for at least five years. In addition, they should not be eligible for citizenship until they speak English, can pass a test in English, can prove that they do not have a criminal record, and have found gainful employment no matter how meager. In America, you can always move up.

In a January 21st, 2005 interview by CNN News, a migrant labor organizer in Long Island, NY asserted that illegal alien workers are being *forced* to work as slaves. However, unlike the African slaves brought to our country 150 years ago, these immigrant workers are not being *forced* to come here. We need to teach respect for the fact that U.S. citizenship is *an honor and a privilege*, not a right or a convenience. This is not a platitude; it is an irrefutable fact that those fortunate enough to reside in the United States of America need to keep in mind. We have made a mockery out of the honor of gaining citizenship in this country by naturalizing virtually anyone, even if they do not speak English – our national language; and then we wonder why there is such disunity, feelings of disenfranchisement, scorn, and factionalism throughout the land. Factions are a natural part of society, but factionalism is not; factionalism is a societal poison that leads to fanaticism.

It is one thing to protect our citizens' rights, but it is quite another to extend that protection to illegals who are not likely to respect the values of our nation or the privileges that come to them without being earned. A sad case in point is Zacarias Moussaoui, the convicted hijacker who wanted to "learn how to steer a plane" but did not care about taking off or landing. We arrested him but felt prevented from looking at the contents of his laptop. Had we done so, the World Trade Center and the Pentagon building, as well as countless lives at home and abroad, might very well have been saved.

A GOVERNOR'S PLAN TO DESTROY AMERICA

Former three-term Colorado Governor, Richard D. Lamm offered his take on the current immigration brouhaha in an article published by, and reprinted here with the permission of, *American Conservative* magazine, titled *"How to Destroy a Nation,"* (March 14, 2006). Governor Lamm is currently a University Professor and Co-Director of the Institute for Public Policy Studies and Executive Director of the Center for Public Policy & Contemporary Issues.

"I Have a Plan to Destroy America

I have a secret plan to destroy America. If you believe, as many do, that America is too smug, too white bread, too self-satisfied, too rich, lets destroy America. It is not that hard to do. History shows that nations are more fragile than their citizens think. No nation in history has survived the ravages of time. Arnold Toynbee observed that all great civilizations rise and they all fall, and that "An autopsy of history would show that all great nations commit suicide." Here is my plan:

I. We must first make America a bilingual-bicultural country. History shows, in my opinion, that no nation can survive the tension, conflict, and antagonism of two competing languages and cultures. It is a blessing for an individual to be bilingual; it is a curse for a society to be bilingual. One scholar, Seymour Martin Lipset, put it this way:

The histories of bilingual and bicultural societies that do not assimilate are histories of turmoil, tension, and tragedy. Canada, Belgium, Malaysia, Lebanon—all face crises of national existence in which minorities press for autonomy, if not independence. Pakistan and Cyprus have divided. Nigeria suppressed an ethnic rebellion. France faces difficulties with its Basques, Bretons, and Corsicans.

II. I would then invent "multiculturalism" and encourage immigrants to maintain their own culture. I would make it an article of belief that all cultures are equal: that there are no cultural differences that are important. I would declare it an article of faith that the Black and Hispanic dropout rate is only due to prejudice and discrimination by the majority. Every other explanation is out-of-bounds.

III. We can make the United States a "Hispanic Quebec" without much effort. The key is to celebrate diversity rather than unity. As Benjamin Schwarz said in the *Atlantic Monthly* recently:

...the apparent success of our own multiethnic and multicultural experiment might have been achieved not by tolerance but by hegemony. Without the dominance that once dictated ethnocentrically, and what it meant to be an American, we are left with only tolerance and pluralism to hold us together.

I would encourage all immigrants to keep their own language and culture. I would replace the melting pot metaphor with a salad bowl metaphor. It is important to insure that we have various cultural sub-groups living in America reinforcing their differences rather than Americans, emphasizing their similarities.

IV. Having done all this, I would make our fastest growing demographic group the least educated – I would add a second underclass, unassimilated, undereducated, and antagonistic to our population. I would have this second underclass have a 50% drop out rate from school.

V. I would then get the big foundations and big business to give these efforts lots of money. I would invest in ethnic identity, and I would establish the cult of Victimology. I would get all minorities to think their lack of success was all the fault of the majority – I would start a grievance industry blaming all minority failure on the majority population.

VI. I would establish dual citizenship and promote divided loyalties. I would "celebrate diversity." "Diversity" is a wonderfully seductive word. It stresses differences rather than commonalities. Diverse people worldwide are mostly engaged in hating each other—that is, when they are not killing each other. A diverse," peaceful, or stable society is against most historical precedent. People undervalue the unity it takes to keep a nation together, and we can take advantage of this myopia. Look at the ancient Greeks. Dorf's *World History* tells us:

The Greeks believed that they belonged to the same race; they possessed a common language and literature; and they worshiped the same gods. All Greece took part in the Olympic games in honor of Zeus and all Greeks venerated the shrine of Apollo at Delphi. A common enemy Persia threatened their liberty. Yet, all of these bonds together were not strong enough to overcome two factors... (local patriotism and geographical conditions that nurtured political divisions...)

If we can put the emphasis on the "Pluribus," instead of the "Unum," we can balkanize America as surely as Kosovo.

VII. Then I would place all these subjects off limits – make it taboo to talk about. I would find a word similar to "Heretic" in the 16th century – that stopped discussion and paralyzed thinking. Words like "racist", "xenophobe" that halts argument and conversation.

Having made America a bilingual-bicultural country, having established multiculturalism, having the large foundations fund the doctrine of "Victimology", I would next make it impossible to enforce our immigration laws. I would develop a mantra – "that because immigration has been good for America, it must always be good." I would make every individual immigrant sympatric and ignore the cumulative impact.

VIII. Lastly, I would censor Victor Davis Hanson's book Mexifornia – this book is dangerous -- it exposes my plan to destroy America. So please, please – if you feel that America deserves to be destroyed –Please, please – don't buy this book! This guy is on to my plan."

****

I will close this chapter with a humorous, but telling, piece that has been floating around the Internet. While Mexico is the subject country it could apply to any nation whose people trample our immigration laws and public laws of conduct:

"Try this:
Enter Mexico illegally. Never mind immigration quotas, visas, international law, or any of that nonsense.

Once there, demand that the local government provide free medical care for you and your entire family. Demand bilingual nurses and doctors.

Demand free bilingual local government forms, bulletins, etc.

Procreate abundantly beyond your means of support. Deflect any criticism of this allegedly irresponsible reproductive behavior with, 'It is a cultural U.S.A. Thing. You would not understand, pal.'

Keep your American identity strong. Fly Old Glory from your rooftop, or proudly display it in your front window or on your car bumper.

Speak only English at home and in public and insist that your children do likewise.

Demand classes on American culture in the Mexican school system.

Demand a local Mexican driver's license. This will afford other legal rights and will go far to legitimize your unauthorized, illegal, presence in Mexico.

Drive around with no liability insurance and ignore local traffic laws.

Insist that local Mexican law enforcement teach English to all its officers.

Good luck! You'll be demanding until the end of time because it will never happen. It will not happen in Mexico or any other country in the world except right here in the United States; land of the naive and stupid and idiotic, politically correct, politicians.

If you agree, pass it on. If you don't, go ahead and try the above in Mexico or Iraq."

CHAPTER 10

HEALTHCARE

The care of human life and happiness, and not their destruction, is the first and only legitimate object of good government.
Thomas Jefferson

Healthcare is the largest and most expensive industry in America. According to investment bank Welsh, Carson, Anderson and Stowe:

> "National health expenditures in the United States rose to $1.6 trillion in 2002, growing 6% faster than the overall economy. [They] are projected to reach $3.1 trillion by 2012, representing an annual growth rate of over 7%... The healthcare industry is undergoing substantial change as a result of government and private sector efforts to decrease costs, increase access and improve the quality of services. The industry is expected to continue to grow, given the demographics of an aging U.S. population, technological developments that prolong life and political forces that provide universal access to the healthcare system."

Healthcare is about more than one's individual well-being. As the largest expenditure (other than homes) that any of us make, healthcare is a matter of national defense that must be addressed by a government that can operate efficiently and with maximum efficacy. Just as an army needs to be healthy in order to defend its country, so, too, does its citizenry – the people who work to make our country work – need to be in the best condition possible. We need to stop wasting so much of our national income on highly inefficient healthcare so that we can at least maintain parity with fast-growing industrial and economic competition from the European Union and the "Asian Tigers." One by one, out-of-control healthcare costs are pulling down venerable institutions that have employed us and fed the lifeblood of our economy. The largest, General Motors "G.M.," is teetering on the brink of extinction. An old saying, "What's good for General Motors is good for America," is a two-edged sword. Hemorrhaging literally billions of dollars of red ink, in March of 2006 G.M. "bit the bullet" and announced that it would be less expensive to spend $2 Billion to buy out all 113,000 of its U.S.-based union employees than it would to make good on their future retirement program. As *The New York Times* opined ("What's Bad for G.M.," March 24, 2006):

> "[G.M.'s] troubles are the embodiment of our fears. G.M. worsens the nagging worry about an America without the kinds of jobs that can provide the salaries needed to support families, good health care and a secure retirement...Soaring health care costs are a competitive disaster ... If the country shudders at the idea of giving up on G.M. it should really fear the structural problems facing employers, from local governments and small businesses to conglomerates. We can turn away and avoid those problems for a bit longer, or tackle them head-on. That will require political bravery in Washington, always a precious rarity."

Don't count on that bravery coming from Washington until things get so bad that Congressional action will be too little too late. We-the-People must save our selves. The DayLight Forum is a good place to start.

It's not just big conglomerates. People all over America, regardless of their education or income level, in large or small businesses and even government jobs, are finding that they cannot afford healthcare. We can no longer attribute this to some personal failing on their part. It is distinctly a matter of decades of Congresses being asleep at the switch with regard to the immediate and forecasted needs of their constituents. And yet, "the man or woman on the street" saw it coming but, apathetically, did not take action to cause the people who they elected to look out for them. We must take that voting power back.

We cannot continue to let people die in massive numbers because our elected leaders cannot come to a logical and fair consensus about a workable national healthcare policy. We are already paying for those of us who cannot pay. The hospitals that treat them pass the cost on to those who *can* pay in the form of higher charges and/or, if they are a for-profit institution, to the government by writing off losses against their income tax bill. So, if we are going to end up paying for it anyway, we might as well face the challenge head-on and get the best possible care; but first we must address the reasons that healthcare is so expensive. A good place to start is to put to rest the myth that doctors and lawyers are the cause of skyrocketing healthcare expenses.

Bad doctors and frivolous lawsuits account for less than 2% of the total-cost problem facing us today. PriceWaterhouse Coopers estimates that the cost of litigation and malpractice adds about 1% to the cost of healthcare premiums; this makes up 7% ($5 Billion) of the overall increase in premium costs. The plain truth is that rising healthcare costs are due to four factors:

- Large hospital chains with huge appetites for revenue feel tremendous pressure to inflate prices and, in too many instances, to defraud both government and private payment sources. Numerous press reports, including a March 5, 2006 segment on CBS' *60-Minutes* "Hospitals: Is the Price Right?" have described a widespread practice of hospitals charging uninsured patients – the ones who can afford it the least – three to five times, and as much as ten times, what they charge insured patients.

- Pharmaceutical companies, by and large, do not cure diseases; they treat *symptoms*, thereby ensuring a reliable, virtually never-ending, source of cash flow, which is needed to recoup the tremendous cost of gaining FDA approval and spending billions of dollars on needless, often dangerously misleading, advertisements on television and in print media.

- Government rules prevent employer groups from banding together for the purpose of obtaining volume discounts on healthcare insurance and medicine.

- Too many patients, including virtually all of the illegal alien class, who cannot or do not pay.

With regard to malpractice, no one has the right to legislate your right to redress for being deprived of life, liberty, and happiness. So-called "tort reform" is just another example of Big Money and special interest lobbies ganging up on the individual citizen: in this case, denying his or her constitutional right to legal redress. Doctors and nurses do not need to practice defensive medicine, just conscientious medicine.

"DRIVER'S LICENSES" FOR DOCTORS AND LAWYERS

While bad doctors and dishonest lawyers are not the primary reason for sky-rocketing medical costs, they still cost us money. The practical solution to frivolous malpractice litigation and consequential high insurance costs, and the way to save lives, is to institute a *points system* for medical licenses, like that which we have for driver's licenses. Particularly egregious offenses, like being drunk or otherwise impaired while treating a patient, would automatically trigger revocation of the offender's license to practice. If we apply this kind of "tough love" to pilots, why not doctors? If a frivolous lawsuit is brought, hold the patient and their lawyer liable. Apply the same driver's license metric to the lawyer and fine the lawyer's malpractice insurance. We-the-People have learned that we cannot leave it up to our elected leaders (many of whom are lawyers), corrupted as they are by special interest groups like the pharmaceutical industry, to make hard decisions that need to be made *now*. This simple points system will take the onus off innocent, honest people who are harmed each year and put it squarely on the shoulders of the patients, medical providers, and lawyers who try to game the system.

> **If you think health care is expensive now, wait until you see what it costs when it's free.** *P.J. O'Rourke*

National healthcare does not have to go the way of our bloated, ineffectual, illogical, and oft-corrupted government bureaucracy. There already exists a highly effective private industry watchdog, which provides a quality and cost-control service that is remarkably effective. It is called Utilization Review and Case Management "UR") and it is quietly saving significant amounts of money for the 65-70% of Corporate America that self-insures their employee health plans. The UR industry can easily extend this service to a public program that covers pre-certification, in-hospital stay review, after-care services, billing review and treatment audits, and disease and long-term case management, including remote nurse telemonitoring as described below. The UR industry has proven that it can serve two masters: the patients, by ensuring that they receive the best possible care; and the payer, by ensuring that the right care and proper billing is applied (e.g. not billing $10 for an aspirin or billing a mother of newborn triplets for four hospital room television rentals). On a national average, UR firms save their self-insuring clients three dollars for every dollar spent. Can you imagine how much more effective such a program would be if UR were organized, rather than utilized in the highly fragmented, company-by-company environment that it is today?

The combination of experienced private oversight and a technologically savvy government program that brings paper records, prescriptions, and payments into a single, coordinated, open-architecture format will ensure that healthcare is delivered in the most effective manner possible. Healthcare presents yet another value proposition and reason to place our government and critical services on an easily accessible Internet platform – a platform whose prototype could conceivably be developed on the DayLight Forum's Internet platform. The move to the Internet is already starting, in a small way, with a phenomenon called "Remote nurse telemonitoring" – a process that is already reducing the cost of expensive conventional home nursing visits as much as 80%.

Remote telemonitoring has become so sophisticated that it can tell a nurse, at a central station a thousand miles away, your blood pressure; whether you are experiencing congestive heart failure or have gained weight; it can read blood gases without pricking your finger; and perform literally dozens of other measurements that can improve and extend life. At roughly $7-10 per day versus a nurse's visit at $50-150 per day, you have the beginning of an economically viable health system. Add tangible rewards for individualized preventive healthcare (e.g. eating right, exercising, eliminating or moderating vices, excessive behavior and risk-taking) and we will become a nation that is stronger and more able to compete on the world stage.

We have become an overindulging, overweight, out-of-shape nation ready to be surpassed by leaner, hungrier, international competitors who have never been as spoiled as we have become. A healthier We-the-People can more readily press forward with the process of cleansing our nation's collective soul – one that has been compromised by the lies of Big Money and special interest groups.

ONE BAD IDEA ON TOP OF ANOTHER

Health savings accounts and consumer-directed health plans are a bad idea for the same reason that privatized Social Security is a bad idea: too many of our fellow citizens will not have the discipline or ability to maintain their program, so they will be left without coverage. Too much money and manpower will have to be spent on the administrative cost of keeping track of these private accounts – perhaps the same "10 to 30 times" cost projection associated with administering President Bush's proposed privatized Social Security system.

More than 40% of Americans can no longer afford adequate medical care and 45 million of us are uninsured. In a *New York Times* article ("Newt Gingrich: Health Care's Unlikely Surgeon," January 16, 2005), former House Speaker Gingrich opined that separating the class of people who can afford healthcare from those who cannot ends up, "penalizing sick people by making their insurance more expensive and harder to obtain. That may just increase the burden on community hospitals, states and the federal government." While much of what Mr. Gingrich is touting in the healthcare field is admirable (e.g. preventative medicine and bringing a paper-based medical industry into the 21st century), his view on emphasizing the role of individual choice and responsibility is too idealistic and has been proven to be contrary to demonstrated human behavior.

The same article paraphrases Mr. Gingrich's position on the only choice for millions of us today: "The higher the deductible, the lower the insurance premiums. Make your choice, take your bet, live with the consequences." That is no way for us to treat one another. An individual is made up of millions of cells. One sick cell can take a person down perhaps permanently. Likewise, a nation is made up of millions of people and, just as illness and injury can take down an individual, so, too, can poor health take down a nation if left to proliferate on a broad scale. To paraphrase Ben Franklin:

"For want of a nail a shoe was lost. For want of a shoe a horse was lost. For want of a horse a king was lost. For want of a king a battle and a nation were lost." Healthcare reform is a battle that none of us can afford to lose.

CHAPTER 11

EDUCATION

In February 2006 I witnessed a thousand-person march around the White House by an anti-war, anti-Bush, group called "The World Can't Wait." Standing in the rain on the side of Constitution Avenue were 5 or 6 young people holding up handmade signs in support of the President. One in particular caught my eye. It read, **"Our soldiers are building schools in Iraq."**

It is sobering to think of how many new schools, how many teacher salaries, how many extracurricular programs could have been funded with the $1 Trillion that has been wasted on Iraq – a nation that, for the most part, detests us and, contrary to the claims of the Bush administration, did not attack us or pose an "imminent threat." The Iraq debacle is bleeding into many areas of our domestic life, and education is no exception. We are kidding ourselves if we think we can change a theocratic Iraqi culture to one that embraces democracy and America itself. We are wasting our children's education on a cause that is not ours.

With regard to our country and its value system, there is something seriously wrong with a culture that will shell out $5 million to pay Michael Jackson to do a television commercial aimed at influencing young people to consume a soft drink (which he refused to actually consume) but cannot find the money to reward the people to whom we entrust our children during their formative years. Some states are adopting merit pay systems and replacing tenure. The almost universal response from parents with whom I have spoken is that they like the concept of merit pay for teachers and that tenure can still be a good thing *if* it is tied to performance that is well-defined and measurable.

EDUCATION – A CRUCIAL PART OF NATIONAL DEFENSE

"Knowledge is Power." The freest and most advanced nations are the most educated nations. Like good healthcare, education is as much a part of our national defense as our military. Excerpts from an article ("Scientific Savvy? In U.S., Not Much") that appeared in the August 30th 2005 edition of *The New York Times* highlight this need:

"Dr. Jon D. Miller, a political scientist who directs the Center for Biomedical Communications at the Northwestern University Medical School in Chicago studies how much Americans know about science and what they think about it. His findings are not encouraging.

While scientific literacy has doubled over the past two decades, only 20 to 25 percent of Americans are 'scientifically savvy and alert,' he said in an interview. Most of the rest 'don't have a clue.' At a time when science permeates debates on everything from global warming to stem cell research, he said, people's inability to understand basic scientific concepts undermines their ability to take part in the democratic process.

Only about 10 percent know what radiation is. One adult American in five thinks the Sun revolves around the Earth, an idea science had abandoned by the 17th century.

Today, he asks about topics like the workings of DNA in the cell because 'if you don't know what a cell is, you can't make sense of stem cell research.'

Dr. Miller, who was raised in Portsmouth, Ohio, when it was a dying steel town, attributes much of the nation's collective scientific ignorance to poor education, particularly in high schools. Many colleges require every student to take some science, but most Americans do not graduate from college. And science education in high school can be 'spotty,' he said.

'This country cannot finance good school systems on property taxes,' he said. 'We don't get the best people for teaching because we pay so little. For people in the sciences particularly, if you have some skill, the job market is so good that teaching is not competitive.'"

We need to raise the starting pay of teachers to the same level as that of someone who graduates from law school. This single act will attract those who would otherwise not consider teaching, and will encourage them to participate in a healthy competition that will raise the performance bar. Once we commit ourselves to valuing knowledge more than the spoils of war and the short-term, instant gratification of revenge and profits generated by the military-industrial complex, a powerful and dynamic change in our society can occur. Where will we get the money for such salaries? A better-educated population is a more productive and creative population, which will, in turn, increase our gross national product, thereby providing the wherewithal to fund this elegantly circular economic equation.

We can no longer rest on our past laurels and simply count on America's reputation as "a place of freedom and opportunity" to provide a competitive advantage on the international playing field. Europe and the rising "Asian Tigers" are fast catching up and, in some markets, moving ahead. Foster a generation of better-educated American kids and *they* will figure out what we need to remain competitive globally.

To those who claim that we cannot afford to pay teachers at a level that is competitive with other white-collar professions, there are figures that say otherwise. "America's Learning Deficit," by Henry Levin and Nigel Holmes, featured in the November 7, 2005 issue of *The New York Times*, stated the following:

> **"The costs of a poor education:**
> A high school dropout earns about $260,000 less over a lifetime (present value in current dollars) than a graduate and pays about $60,000 less in taxes. With 23 million high school dropouts between the ages of 18 and 67, that means the federal and state governments lose more than $50 billion in taxes. America forgoes $192 billion, or 1.6% of gross domestic product, in combined income and tax revenue a year with each group of 18-year olds who never complete high school. Increasing the educational attainment of those groups by one year would recoup nearly half of those losses. The average 45-year old high school dropout is in worse health than the average 65-year old high school graduate. High school dropouts have a life expectancy that is 9.2 years shorter than graduates.
>
> **The saving of a good education:**
> America could save $7.9 billion to $10.8 billion annually by improving educational attainment among recipients of Temporary Assistance for Needy Families, food stamps and housing assistance and thereby removing many of them from the rolls. Because high school graduates are less likely to commit crimes, increasing the high school completion rate by just 1% for all men ages 20 to 60 would *reduce costs in the criminal justice system by as much as $1.4 billion per year.* A one-year increase in average years of schooling for dropouts would reduce

> murder and assault by almost 30%, motor vehicle theft by 20%, arson by 13%, and burglary and larceny by about 6%. Participation in model preschool programs has been shown to increase academic achievement, reduce dropout rates and lower the risk of teenage pregnancy, drug use and criminal violence. The economic benefits of such programs are as high as **$7 for each dollar invested.**"

With these obvious benefits, is it not our civic duty to reform education in America? We need to create an educational system that engages students and teachers alike. We can start by limiting class size to 20 students or less instead of packing them in what are often nothing more than cramped, depressing, "holding pens" until they reach the legal age to quit or graduate unable to read or write.

Real-world rules of marketing and sales apply here. Teachers must realize that their students are not captives; they are *customers*. Just as the learning environment is important from the students' standpoint, it is equally important for the teaching environment to give our educators a fair shot at professional and financial success. Put this kind of system in place and, for the majority of students, we will see bad behavior and truancy become a thing of the past.

If we can spend money on war, we can spend it on teachers and books – a much better application of our national assets. Nothing sharpens competition among teachers, or any professional for that matter, like money on the table. The adage "you get what you pay for" has never been truer. We do not need to fear that people will come to teaching just for the money. A fair merit review, accountability and measurement system will ensure that and send a message to prospective entrants that the barrier to *remain* in teaching is also high. Better teachers will turn out better citizens and contributors to our gross domestic product.

The 21st century demands far more than a high school education. The importance of a strong knowledge and skill base must be instilled at an early age. Welfare payments have proven to be insufficient to help people move up out of poverty and criminality. Thus, education must be a requisite part of any public assistance program.

Why do we put our children's future in the hands of some parents who may love them but do not possess the mindset or skills to instill a thirst for knowledge and financial betterment? The old saying, "You need a license to have a dog a but anyone can have a child," may be harsh but, for too many children, it hits close to home. Too many people failed to receive a good education, not because they were not industrious or proactive, but because they had to rely on a mindset and example set by their parents.

While we do not have to advocate an Orwellian takeover of America's children, we can no longer leave their future in the hands of parents who are not motivated or financially able to provide an education that will permit their child to achieve his or her highest potential. We-the-People must give *all* children a uniform opportunity to receive a great education or we will not remain a great nation. We must accentuate civics and the practical realities of daily finance in the curriculum, so that they understand how the world works and are prepared for the onslaught of credit offers, get-rich-quick schemes and schemers that have pulled so many good people down. A generation so educated will not fall prey to things like the Bush administration's ham-handed campaign to take away their Social Security.

One of the planks that we should consider for The DayLight Movement's platform will be an adaptation of a program proposed by British Prime Minister Tony Blair. Anyone who wants to attend college or trade school, but cannot afford it, will be empowered to do so and can then pay their tuition upon graduation via a mandated automatic deduction from their monthly paycheck. Under this program, a teenager's future and the financial load of higher education is in his or her hands rather than in the hands of parents who cannot afford, or do not appreciate, the value of a good education.

Somewhere amongst We-the-People are the minds and wills to make all of this a reality. We just need a place to be heard and responded to with action and money that is currently being wasted overseas and on immoral pork projects. The DayLight Forum is that place and that platform. Great education today will ensure a healthy crop of future leaders for a safer, better, America.

CHAPTER 12

ENERGY

Nothing happens without energy. Our bodies cannot function without energy, which we take in from food that is largely produced here in the good old USA. When we acquire it outside our borders it is largely because it can be produced less expensively, but the important thing to keep in mind is that, if we had to, we could produce it here. In other words, we are "food-independent" of the rest of the world. We cannot say that about oil: a depleting, antiquated, fuel that we depend on foreign sources to provide. Without it, our economy and way of life would not merely stop – we would be plunged into chaos, depression, anarchy, and bloodshed beyond anything in recorded history.

Think about it: no cars on the road; no trucks delivering food and other essentials; many hospitals, power plants and manufacturers shut down; vast sections of the predominately oil furnace-using Northeast without heat, people (not just the poor) freezing and starving. The aftermath of Hurricanes Katrina and Rita is a precursor of what could very well occur, sooner rather than later.

The effects of our precarious oil supply situation reverberate throughout virtually every aspect of American civilization. As of May 2006, the price of gasoline had doubled since President Bush was elected. That increase is not hitting us only at the gas pump. Just one example: the cost of fuel to heat, cool and cook is a major expense for restaurants. If you own a diner and need to raise prices to offset the cost of fuel to operate your business, you could be making yourself less competitive with other diners in your area. That could result in a loss of business, laying off employees or even closing down. Your children may not get to go to college or to attend the school of their choice. You may not be able to take a vacation, which will affect the travel and recreation industries.

We have ignored the eventuality of permanent oil shortages for over a hundred years; we have not built a new oil refinery in the United States in 30 years. Thanks to having stirred up an Islamic hornet's nest with our forced displacement of Arab landowners from Palestine in 1948 and our ongoing imperialistic behavior, we have given life to a fanatic element that would love to disrupt oil production and transmission to all Western nations. China is already setting off alarm bells in India and Europe by competing for Russian and Venezuelan oil. Canada is still our major supplier of oil, natural gas and electricity but no one knows how long it can continue to satisfy our thirst for more and more energy or if terrorists will hit their pipelines into the U.S. Russia now provides so much of Europe's oil that it could turn off the lights anytime it wants. Of course, that would be economic suicide for Russia, but not for the kind of radical fanatics alluded to above.

The story of natural gas is no better: an *AP News* report dated January 22, 2005 ("U.S. Importing More Liquefied Natural Gas") quoted Guy Caruso, head of the government's Energy Information Administration, as saying:

> "[i]f current trends continue, the United States by far will be the largest consumer of LNG in the next decade. If we don't have the capacity to bring in the amount of gas we need and domestic supply goes the way we think it will, the clear implication is higher prices."

> The article went on to quote energy consultant Daniel Yergin, chairman of Cambridge Energy Research Associates:

> "We have not been able to increase gas production for a decade. U.S. gas productive capacity, like oil, is now in permanent decline. Canada's and Mexico's gas fields are also in decline."

FANATIC TERROR: A NEW FACTOR IN THE ENERGY EQUATION

Even if we can ensure a reliable supply from overseas, LNG tankers and storage facilities are ripe and easy terror targets. While LNG cannot explode and is not flammable as a liquid, the *AP* report went on to say that:

> "... a government study by the Sandia National Laboratory concludes terrorists could blast a large hole into a double-hulled LNG vessel. That would release millions of gallons of fuel that would quickly turn to gas and ignite. The fire would be so intense that it could cause major injury and burn buildings one-third of a mile away. Within seconds, the fire could give second-degree burns to people who are a mile away."

That sounds like a holocaust waiting to happen. Clearly, fanatic terror is a new factor in the energy equation. While we're on the topic of fanatic terror and energy, if we weren't so dependent on the Middle East for oil, I wonder if we would have such a presence over there; a presence that is a perpetual "thorn" in the side of the people of the Middle East and that was, in large part, a catalyst for the devastating attacks on American military barracks in Lebanon and Saudi Arabia and the attack on our very soil on September 11th. When will our leaders get the message that America's brand of forced imperial democratization and desire to control oil is not welcome?

While multi-billion dollar initiatives to promote stem cell technology, like that enacted in California, are admirable, any advancement in our quality of life will mean nothing if the lights go out. We-the-People need to get our priorities straight. The $1 Trillion that we have already spent trying to save Iraqi citizens (who should be fighting their own battles) and another $100 Billion chasing a single man on kidney dialysis in Afghanistan could have accelerated a robust alternate energy research program that would make us less reliant on countries run by ruthless dictatorships, such as the Saudi royal family and Vladimir Putin's sham democracy in Russia. There will always be a market for oil, but let it be for the production of *products* like medicine and polymer plastics that must have oil in their recipe.

A strong alternate energy R&D program may eventually replace even many oil-based medical needs through technology that can be developed and commercialized with adequate government support, rather than dithering, debate and grandstanding by politicians who are trying to impress their oil-industry financial masters. The Bush Administration appears to have no problem giving oil companies multibillion dollar tax breaks but God forbid that we should give alternate energy programs the same preference so they can attract the immense amount of capital required to bring new methods, technologies, products and services to commercialization.

Bottom line: We-the-People need to face the fact that we are all living on borrowed energy time based on a depleting fuel that is dramatically affecting global climate and the environment of literally all living species. Whatever value there may be in getting foreign oil producers to increase production is nothing more than a short-term fix to a larger, long-term problem.

There is, however, an interesting counterpoint to this. The following article comes from a newsletter for investors (*Rational Investor*, April 2005):

"The Myth of Expensive Oil

The reasons for high gas prices are well-known and pretty much agreed on. And each one is dead wrong, as you'll see.

- We're running out. We're entering a New Dark Age, a chilly post Petroleum Era.
- Demand is exceeding supply – largely because of China's growth.
- Terrorists are disrupting supplies – and plan to take control of Saudi oil fields any day now.
- The Russian oil business is in turmoil, and exports could be cut off.

Wrong on all counts.

- Oil production has not peaked, nor is it declining. Dozens of giant oil fields have been discovered in the past few years. What's more, all are outside the tinderbox of the Middle East. One day we will run out, but that day, according to every geologist who is not on the lunatic fringe, is 25 generations from now. Then, perhaps, we'll all be huddled under windmills (or, more likely, we'll be using free hydrogen power).
- Increase in demand is running at around 3 million barrels a day, but increase in supply is running at 3.5 million barrels, according to the International Energy Agency. This half a million barrels a day excess supply situation has not changed – in the last 8 years. Even a mild tap on the brakes from China (growth recently slowed 25%, by the way), and we'd be up to our necks in oil!
- Terrorists are a non-issue. While the media are giving outages great coverage, production in the Middle East has been steadier than at any time in the last 5 years. The chance of a major, prolonged disruption by terrorists of oil supplies is very low. Even if terrorists were successful, OPEC's own strategic reserves alone could cover global demand for the next two years!
- China's sopping up all the oil. IN FACT, China is an almost insignificant part of the pricing equation for oil.
- Terrorists are shutting down Mideast oil fields. IN FACT, supply from the region has been more consistent – and consistently strong – than at any time in the last 10 years. The last significant disruption of oil supplies tied to terrorism occurred before 9/11!

- Terrorists might shut down Mideast oil fields. IN FACT, the odds are rationally calculated at one-in-twenty. These odds are worth perhaps as much as a one dollar premium on the price of oil (not $15–$20).
- But you don't KNOW that! IN FACT, we do know that we have taken the fight to the terrorists. We have hunted them out, pinned them down, and taken them out. We are safer for that – and our oil supplies are, too. Terrorism will always be a threat. But now it is a contained threat.
- Inventories are dangerously low. That has to keep prices high. IN FACT, inventories of 300 million barrels are consistent with $28 a barrel oil.
- High oil prices are an accepted part of life in Europe. Now it's our turn. IN FACT, high oil prices in Europe are caused by socialist policies, a massive tax burden, government pending and a dense thicket of regulations. In 1991, after the first Gulf War, oil fell 34% to $26.40 in the U.S. And a few weeks ago, oil crashed 12% in 2 days, giving Rational Investors like us a taste of what's to come in 2005.
- The world's running out of oil! IN FACT, Saudi Arabia has just boosted production by 14% and vows to keep a spare capacity of 1.5 million barrels a day over and above production. To ensure that Saudi sheiks stay in power, they plan to double output in the next few years. OPEC needs price volatility to satisfy its opposing objectives of higher revenues and market share. But beyond the volatility – there's plenty of oil.
- The promised oil from Iraq will never arrive. IN FACT, Iraq is capa ble of pumping 6 million barrels a day. The Saudis would rather they didn't – and the best way to make sure is by dropping oil's price to a point where the world (especially the U.S.) decides not to bother restoring Iraq's oil infrastructure."

So whom do we believe? We will know with markedly greater surety when We-the-People convene with the best and brightest at the DayLight Forum.

CHAPTER 13

RELIGION AND SPIRITUALITY

"If there were no God, there would be no Atheists." *G.K. Chesterton*

To paraphrase and add a bit more to an old Bible saying, "Wherever two or more of us are gathered in His name, there is love" – and hypocrisy, violence, bloodshed and war; all in the name of religion and its poison aspect: religious intolerance.

The majority of We-the-People are against the tolerance of religious intolerance. This includes Islam, Judaism, and Christianity in their radical forms. Sooner or later, we are going to have to face the fact that not all religious beliefs can be tolerated. If a religion preaches that its followers should kill non-believers, then we need to root them out because they present a danger to the common good – even to members of their own faith. If you find a snake under your living room sofa, you don't let it stay there. If troublemakers, religious or not, want to identify themselves by their headscarf, tattoos, or gang colors, then that's great – "thanks for helping us identify you, now get the hell out of here."

Am I religiously tolerant? Let's see, if you're a Christian and you take or condone the taking of land in a cruel way from the American Indians; if you're a Jew and you believe that you can take people's land by force and then punish them and call them terrorists for fighting back against overwhelming forces financed by others; if you're a Muslim and you believe that all Christians and Jews should be killed, then I'm prejudiced and intolerant. If you're a Christian who believes that we should love our neighbors (and enemies) as we love ourselves; if you're a Jew who respects the wonderful guidance of the Talmud; if you're a Muslim and you respect the beautiful tenets of your religion and of other religions, then I'm neither prejudiced nor intolerant.

It is an undeniable fact that America was founded on a strong belief in God. To deny that now would be to deny the fact that all great civilizations have been built on a similar foundation consisting of a rich mix of tradition, oral and written history, practice, and repetition – all cemented by faith, and hardened and cured by the test of time. To suddenly attack that foundation, even if it is to remove just one of the above-referenced ingredients, in this case *faith*, would be tantamount to taking the sand out of cement or removing the supporting foundation from under a hundred-story building. What is going to replace it? What will hold that proverbial building up, and how vulnerable will it be while the switch to secularism is made? Even with all its faults, the United States is the greatest, wealthiest, and most powerful nation in the history of the world. Is undermining its foundation worth the risk and effort?

> **"A simple way to take measure of a country is to look at how many want in and how many want to get out."** *Prime Minister Tony Blair*

Just as you would not mess with a building's foundation, so we should not mess with a great nation's fundamental values. If you do not like our fundamentals, move to a Godless country – if you can find one.

In conversations with a vast cross-section of Americans, it became clear that, for most of us, "Religion' and "God" are related but distinctly different topics. I was surprised at how many told me that, while they may not like it, they can understand an argument about the inappropriateness of having the term "Under God" in something as universal as our Pledge of Allegiance. For them, whether God is in the pledge or not, He will remain where it counts – in the hearts, homes, churches, synagogues, mosques, or other spiritual gathering places of His faithful; and no one will prevent them, as individuals, from continuing to say "under God," if they so desire, when they recite the Pledge. *Obligating* them, they say, to add that phrase is quite another matter.

More than a few Bible scholars point out that the New Testament proscribes public displays of spirituality for the sake of public display alone (Matthew 6:5-6) and that even "swearing by God" as an oath of truth is proscribed (Matthew 5:33-37). Lynn Nofziger, Press Secretary and, later, Assistant to the President for Political Affairs in the Reagan White House, put the issue of God, religion, the First Amendment, and the Constitution in better perspective than anything I could ever write:

> "It's always a source of amazement to me how the courts, the lawyers and the bureaucrats can twist the words of the Constitution to mean anything they want them to mean... Take, for example, the First Amendment, the words of which have been distorted into meaning that God and religion, primarily Christianity, have no place in public

> life and that Christmas itself should be abolished from public schools, public buildings and public places. Yet what does the First Amendment actually say regarding religion? Here it is: 'Congress shall make no law respecting an establishment of religion or prohibiting the free exercise thereof.' That's all it says. After that it talks about free speech, a free press and the right of the people to petition the government. But out of those 16 words regarding the relationship of religion to the government, the courts over the years have steadily issued rulings based on the first 10 words of the amendment and ignoring the last six that go far beyond anything the amendment even hints at. If words mean what they say it seems to me what the amendment is saying is that Congress cannot pass a law that would establish a national religion, be it Christianity, Islam, Baal worship or anything else. And, at the same time, it, meaning Congress, cannot pass a law in any way banning the practice of religion. Seems pretty plain to me."

In mid-February of 2004, U.S. Senator Zell Miller (D-GA) delivered the following statement on the floor of the United States Senate, addressing several social issues facing the country. Excerpted below is his take on the separation of Church and State:

> "Everyone today seems to think that the U.S. Constitution expressly provides for separation of church and state. Ask any ten people if that's not so. And I'll bet you most of them will say "Well, sure." And some will point out, "it's in the First Amendment."
>
> Wrong! Read it! It says, "Congress shall make no law respecting an establishment of religion or prohibiting the free exercise thereof." Where is the word "separate"? Where are the words "church" or "state"?
>
> They are not there. Never have been. Never intended to be. Read the Congressional Records during that four-month period in 1789 when the amendment was being framed in Congress. Clearly their intent was to prohibit a single denomination in exclusion of all others, whether it was Anglican or Catholic or some other."

Both Senator Miller's and Lyn Nofziger's points reinforce the idea that there is room for God in our government.

While I was unable to find data about what percentage of Jews take the Torah or the Bible literally, according to an ABCNEWS/*Primetime* poll conducted in February of 2004 a majority of Christians believe that some of the best-known Bible stories are literally true. Being that it was written by men who were not taking direct dictation it seems reasonable to assume that the Bible is more likely the *inspired* word of God. Thus, we would be wise to use our common sense to determine how to respond to the Bible's messages. This is not "an out" or a blanket permission to do as we please or what is convenient; it is simply a matter of using another gift from God – our brains – to make our choices. This also applies to things like Old Testament claims that the Palestinian land taken in 1948 belongs solely to the Jews, as much as it does to Bible-derived implications that slavery is acceptable. How silly it is to think that, with all the changes that have taken place in the world, the same God has simply stopped sending additional messages over the past two or three thousand years.

ARMAGEDDON DOESN'T HAVE TO HAPPEN

Biblical teachings do not necessarily mandate war. I believe that they are more of a warning than a prediction. For example, if we exercise our God-given freewill and just don't engage in religious wars anymore, we can avoid the dire predictions of Armageddon. The opposite of this is the Bush Administration moronically allowing fanatic religious savages to pull the most enlightened of us into unnecessary conflicts that we think are about democracy and they think are about theology.

To call Bill Moyers a noted journalist would not do justice to an icon of news, information, and journalistic wisdom. Excerpts from an address at Harvard University say much about the troubled mindset of a major portion of our country and how they are twisting the words of the Bible to: justify abuse of the environment; invade sovereign nations on false pretexts; support the 1947 eviction of Arab citizens from their land, which was given to their sworn enemy; continue to support Israel's inhumane treatment of the Palestinian people over the past 58-years; abuse our environment; waste our natural resources; and violate our constitutional rights. The only thing I would humbly add is to say that those who take the Bible literally are ignoring the fact that God gave us free will. That single gift empowers us to move future history in a positive direction. We do not have to follow Biblical predictions that conveniently (and disingenuously) favor the people who wrote them or those who now distort their meaning.

He writes: *"One of the biggest changes in politics in my lifetime is that the delusional is no longer marginal. It has come in from the fringe, to sit in the seat of power in the oval office and in Congress. For the first time in our history, ideology and theology hold a monopoly of power in Washington. Theology asserts propositions that cannot be proven true; ideologues hold stoutly to a world view despite being contradicted by what is generally accepted as reality. When ideology and theology couple, their offspring are not always bad but they are always blind. And there is the danger: voters and politicians alike, oblivious to the facts' ... 'The news is not good these days. I can tell you, though, that as a journalist, I know the news is never the end of the story. The news can be the truth that sets us free - not only to feel but to fight for the future we want. And the will to fight is the antidote to despair, the cure for cynicism' ... 'What we need to match the science of human health is what the ancient Israelites called 'hocma' - the science of the heart...the capacity to see....to feel....and then to act...as if the future depended on you. Believe me, it does."*

****

It is not just Congress and corporations that have lost their way when it comes to solid values and clear thinking. The Catholic Church's move to rush the late Pope John Paul II to sainthood at a time when the Church is reeling from him having turned a blind eye and deaf ear to repeated reports of sexual abuse of children, speaks volumes about how the poison of secularism and selfish lust has pervaded even our most hallowed religious institutions. The following is a letter to the editor, from me, that was published in the *New Canaan Advertiser* on April 21, 2005:

> "As a devout Christian who was raised a Catholic it pains me to write this letter. The massive, at times fawning, coverage of the late Pope John Paul II overlooks a larger point that says much about just how decadent our media-driven, star worshipping, world has become. While this wonderful man's impact on world affairs was certainly positive, and his intentions good and noble, by any definition of the term 'leader' he was an abject failure who turned a blind eye to a pedophiliac poison that flowed through his cavalry of 'Christian soldiers.'

A CEO's job is to establish and promote the values and culture of his or her organization. As the Catholic Church's CEO and a major influencer in the Christian and non-Christian world, he failed to protect a major customer constituency: thousands, perhaps millions, of children who were sodomized, traumatized, and silenced during the time of his reign. What about the young lambs who were raped and then called liars during his tenure as shepherd of the flock? How many dioceses are now bankrupt and closed because of his (and his predecessor's) failure to acknowledge this massive problem years ago? Where was a 'good act of confession?' Who is truly doing penance? By its own admission, the Catholic Church's credibility is at perhaps its lowest point. How does rushing someone to sainthood who failed to protect the '.. little children who come unto Me' raise that credibility?

Falling back on what seems to be a trend among scofflaw CEOs who offer an excuse that they 'didn't know what they didn't know' flies in the face of overwhelming evidence of a century's long cover up and protection of those under his command. The buck should have stopped with him.

Pope John Paul II's refusal to advocate the use of condoms to help stem the holocaust-like loss of life in Africa, and his insistence that families burden themselves with children that they (and the state) cannot afford showed a callous disregard for the economic and social reality of life. A disregard that was forcefully driven home by the choice of Cardinal Bernard Law (former Archbishop of Boston who was forced from office for decades of protecting pedophile priests) as an honored participant in the Pope's funeral. Assuming that the culture and value system that permitted these travesties is the same one that gave Cardinal Law his starring role in the Pope's funeral mass, how can the Church nominate the chief keeper of that system for sainthood? This drum beat for sainthood is about far more than one man. It is a disturbing "canary in the coal mine" about the decadence of our world society and mores – and the Church wonders where its parishioners have gone.

While there is certainly something to be said for the symbolism of a magnificent headquarters, a great CEO would have ensured that some of the money that maintains that palatial Vatican lifestyle would have gone to ensure that his Third World flock at least had clean water, which can be provided to a small village for less than $1,000 and, in some circumstances, for a little as $10. By any measure in the secular world he would have been fired as CEO, but the overwhelming pomp and circumstance of a bureaucracy that is accountable to no one ensures that will never happen (then again, a number of Catholics have voted with their feet). Perhaps the next Pope will switch focus from 'fighting the good fight' on an international political level and get down to cleaning his (or her) own house. 'Rebuild it and they will come.'"

Some final words on religion from a Christian and a Jew:

"Meaning no disrespect to the religious convictions of others, I still can't help wondering how we can explain away what to me is the greatest miracle of all and which is recorded in history. No one denies there was such a man, that he lived and that he was put to death by crucifixion. Where... is the miracle I spoke of? Well consider this and let your imagination translate the story into our own time – possibly to your own hometown. A young man whose father is a carpenter grows up working in his father's shop. One day he puts down his tools and walks out of his father's shop. He starts preaching on street corners and in the nearby countryside, walking from place to place, preaching all the while, even though he is not an ordained minister. He never gets farther than an area perhaps 100 miles wide at the most. He does this for three years. Then he is arrested, tried and convicted. There is no court of appeal, so he is executed at age 33 along with two common thieves. Those in charge of his execution roll dice to see who gets his clothing – the only possessions he has. His family cannot afford a burial place for him so he is interred in a borrowed tomb. End of story? No, this uneducated, property-less young man who... left no written word has, for 2,000 years, had a greater effect on the world than all the rulers, kings, emperors; all the conquerors, generals and admirals; all the scholars, scientists and philosophers who have ever lived – all of them put together. How do we explain that... unless he really was what he said he was?" *Ronald Reagan*

"Christmas is not my holiday. For a practicing Jew, the twenty-fifth of December is no more significant than the twenty-fifth of any other month. But I enjoy the Christmas season a great deal. I appreciate the spirit of generosity and the reflection on religious themes that the holiday engenders, and I love the mood, the music, and even the decorations. Many Jews and other non-Christians may feel a bit "out of it" during the Christmas season, but I have absolutely no problem with such a feeling... Moreover, I enjoy observing Christians celebrate their Christianity. For a Jew rooted in Judaism, Christians rooted in their identity are a blessing, not a problem... What this Jew does dread is an America that ceases to celebrate Christmas." *Dennis Prager*

CHAPTER 14

THE UNITED STATES MILITARY

Military service is no longer just a patriotic function; it has become a catchment for a generation of youth who have been failed by a substandard educational system and an unimaginative labor market that has left them with no place else to go. Young people (and often their parents) with no solid sense of world affairs are susceptible to enticing concepts like "serving your country" and "keeping America safe." At their young age, most think they will live forever, but in reality they are being killed and maimed by the thousands.

Bravado statements and support for the war by some soldiers stationed in Iraq has more to do with a combination of youthful exuberance, fueled by military indoctrination, and the simple camaraderie phenomenon of "Misery loves company." It is time for those of us who are a little more experienced, and have lived through the travesty of Vietnam, to start speaking the unvarnished truth.

What was said in an earlier chapter about respecting and paying our teachers goes for our soldiers as well. The following scenario has been playing out for decades: American soldiers, who also have to work an off-post job to make ends meet, are suddenly called into duty for a year or longer leaving behind families without enough to live on. Their spouses essentially become single parents who have to work while leaving their children in daycare. What kind of society rewards people, who lay their lives on the line for their country, with a pittance of a salary that forces so many to apply for welfare? What kind of leadership sends these same men and women into combat without proper gear? Ridiculously expensive Humvees lacking even minimal armor; cheap, malfunctioning flak jackets; tents and other camouflage gear containing deadly levels of lead paint ("Military Was Sold Lead-Tainted Fabric for Tents" *The New York Times*, March 24, 2004) are just a few examples of the mistreatment of our soldiers.

The egregious failure to properly plan for the military attack and occupation of Iraq is, in and of itself, grounds for impeachment of our leaders and court martial action against our generals. This assertion is reinforced by six generals who, in April of 2006, called for Defense Secretary Rumsfeld's resignation over his failure to manage what should have been a defensive action, not an invasion, against terror. Their ouster call is particularly salient because, as *the New York Times* reported ("More Retired Generals Call for Rumsfeld's Resignation" April 14, 2006) "... the current uproar is significant because Mr. Rumsfeld's critics include generals who were involved in the invasion and occupation of Iraq under the defense secretary's leadership." Even a freshman college history major could have warned our president about the fact that Iraq was another "3-nations within a nation Yugoslavia" waiting to happen and that our invasion would not instill peace much beyond the day that we pull out, if ever.

No one who defends our country should be on food stamps. Instead of spending literally billions of dollars rebuilding a country like Iraq, we need to raise our soldiers' wages and ensure that they and their families are taken care of while they are away on duty. This includes ensuring that they receive more than "adequate" healthcare and rehabilitation when they return. A $2 Billion underestimation of how much is needed to take care of our Iraq War veterans' medical needs screams for the ouster of our failed elected "experts." It's funny how they can find $1 Trillion for a bogus war but not one-twentieth that amount for the soldiers who are bloodied by it. We-the-People need to replace these bunglers with The DayLight Movement's concept of Congressional ombudsmen, who will advise us through a truly democratic, open-book decision-making process – including decisions about war. Some of the best advisors will come from former military leaders who, once they are out from under the threat of censure or demotion, can be relied upon to guide us, candidly and honestly, by serving as one of the new breed of DayLight Congressmen, or as advisors to those Congressmen.

As with teachers, a single act of economic justice will attract those who would otherwise never consider the military, and encourage them to participate in a healthy competition for employment that will further raise the performance bar. A better-paid and better-educated military is a stronger military, and a stronger military breeds a stronger nation. Of course, knowing that there is a better form of governance and decision-making – one that is not manipulated by Big Money interests or the military-industrial complex in such life and death matters – will be an equally powerful recruiting tool.

CHAPTER 15

RACISM

THERE IS NO PLACE ON EARTH FOR IT

> **"I have a dream that one day this nation will rise up and live out the true meaning of its creed: 'We hold these truths to be self-evident, that all men are created equal.' ... I have a dream that my four children will one day live in a nation where they will not be judged by the color of their skin but by the content of their character. ... And if America is to be a great nation this must become true."** *Martin Luther King, Jr.*

How is it that we come out of our mother's womb warm, innocent and loving, only to have some of us become so consumed with cold-blooded hatred that we commit savage acts of violence and neglect against fellow humans whose only "sin" is to be of a different skin color, nationality, political or religious belief?

"Race" is another touchy "PC" subject that can incite as many misguided, knee-jerk, reactions as it does valid ones. A prime example is the observation that, "Relative to the makeup of our national population, a disproportionate percentage of college male and female basketball players are black." Or put another way, "a predominately black basketball team is not representative of the population of its campus." While these statements are true on most college campuses, are they also racially insensitive? Probably not by themselves but when you add the question, "What does that say about our college admissions process?" a "PC" tripwire is triggered and alarm bells start to go off. When I posed this question to a cross-section of Americans, there was no consensus as to where rationality and innocence end and racism starts. We cannot do justice to such a subjective topic within the confines of a single chapter but we can certainly explore it, in detail, in DayLight Forum meetings and face-to-face gatherings across the country. In the meantime, we can touch on a few subjects here just to get the conversational ball rolling.

RACIAL PROFILING

Racial profiling is not racist. Police departments don't profile people simply because of the color of a suspect's skin. Profiling is simply an acknowledgement of the economic fact that a shameful practice of slavery, reinforced by 200 years of abuse and prejudice, has put a significant percentage of our black-skinned fellow citizens in such a collective "hole" that, for those still climbing out, crime is sometimes perceived to be the only way to move up or to survive. If profiling were truly racist, we'd be reading stories of far more Hispanics, Asians and American Indians being pulled over for no good reason. As much as we may not like it (and I do not like it), if the majority of car thefts in a particular area are committed by black citizens, and if drug usage is markedly higher among blacks, wouldn't it be moronic for trained police officers, who often must make split-second decisions, to ignore that data when they see a black person driving the kinds of automobiles that are commonly stolen, or observe them behaving in an erratic manner?

Accusations of racial profiling are not limited to Caucasian police officers. Black officers demonstrate the same observational process; they are being *human*, not racist. Thus, police officers – black, white, yellow or red – should not be punished for making rational inferences based on the very essence of human intelligence i.e., "the ability to cross-reference, compare, and recognize essential similarities between separate subjects or situations." Don't punish policemen for the sins of slave owners and a society that is still finding its way on the subject of race. They're simply doing their job.

On the other hand, our draconian sentencing laws are doing tremendous harm to our country; especially our black youth. For a nation that touts itself as "Godly," we certainly are less forgiving than God. Our jails are filled to overflowing with young people – predominately minorities – who made a bad decision. Who *should* be sentenced are the parents and leaders of our country who have let our society's values and morals decay to such a point of decadence.

NO BLACK MALE LEFT BEHIND – A PERVASIVE SENSE OF HOPELESSNESS

While the Bush Administration touts the success of its "No child left behind" program it is clear that this and previous administrations have egregiously overlooked black males in general, resulting in an already desperate situation that is worsening at an alarming rate. In an in-depth front-page article ("Plight Deepens for Black Men, Studies Warn," March 20, 2006) *The New*

York Times reported that "the huge pool of poorly educated black men are becoming ever more disconnected from the mainstream society, and to a far greater degree than comparable white or Hispanic men." The following factors, some excerpted directly and others paraphrased from the article, tell a story of the greatest nation in the world turning a blind eye to a societal cancer that could have been prevented had we taken action shortly after freeing a race that was dragged here in chains and then spat upon for 200 years:

- According to census data, there are about five million black men ages 20 to 39 in the United States.
- Finishing high school is the exception, legal work is scarcer than ever and prison is almost routine, with incarceration rates climbing for blacks even as urban crime rates have declined.
- In 2004, 72 percent of black male high school dropouts in their 20's were jobless or incarcerated. Even when high school graduates were included, half of black men in their 20's were jobless in 2004, up from 46 percent in 2000.
- As of 2004, 21 percent of black men in their 20's who did not attend college were incarcerated. By their mid-30's, 6 in 10 black men who had dropped out of school had spent time in prison.
- Terrible schools, absent parents, racism, the decline in blue collar jobs and a subculture that glorifies swagger over work have all been cited as causes of the deepening ruin of black youths. Scholars — and the young men themselves — agree that all of these issues must be addressed.
- With the shift from factory jobs, unskilled workers of all races have lost ground, but none more so than blacks. By 2004, 50 percent of black men in their 20's who lacked a college education were jobless, as were 72 percent of high school dropouts, according to data compiled by Bruce Western, a sociologist at Princeton and author of the forthcoming book "Punishment and Inequality in America" *(Russell Sage Press).* These are more than double the rates for white and Hispanic men.
- "By their mid-30's, 30 percent of black men with no more than a high school education have served time in prison, and 60 percent of drop outs have," Mr. Western said.
- Among black dropouts in their late 20's, more are in prison on a given day — 34 percent — than are working — 30 percent — according to

an analysis of 2000 census data by Steven Raphael of the University of California, Berkeley.

- Employment has become almost impossible for young black men in America in part because so many have a prison record, and young blacks with clean records suffer by association. A second special factor is related to an otherwise successful policy: the stricter enforcement of child support: Improved collection of money from absent fathers has been a pillar of welfare overhaul, but the system can leave young men feeling overwhelmed with debt and deter them from seeking legal work, since a large share of any earnings could be seized.

Drawing comparisons with other ethnic groups – especially the rise of Korean immigrants who thrive in predominately black neighborhoods – has become a commonplace response to why so many blacks are in poverty. It is dead wrong. Koreans were not dragged over here in chains and then tainted with the stain of low self-image and low self-esteem that America placed on its former slaves and their descendants. Korean immigrants enter our society from a long national heritage and culture of relatively stable homes and family life, whereas a large segment of today's black youth enter society from a long national heritage of abuse; poverty-ridden, often-fatherless, homes; or as wards of the state.

It is not enough to tell black Americans to "get over it," when we clearly continue to operate a policy of neglect and denial about how things should have been dealt with long ago. We continue to compound our ancestor's sin by failing to provide the kind of training programs and educational opportunities that are needed to pull our black fellow Americans up and out. Every year that we delay doing the right thing makes rectifying it just that much more difficult.

It is more than ironic that our military war strategy is to apply *overwhelming force* to the enemy. Well the *enemy* – i.e. ignorance, crumbling schools, underpaid teachers, and no specialized training oriented to the needs of this important segment of our society – is clearly defined. 10 decades of Congresses have not been able to make more than a dent in this challenge. It is time for We-the-People to take charge and, at risk of using what has become a cliché, "To give not a handout but a hand." It all can start at the DayLight Forum.

FUBU

In the chapter on Israel I cautioned that, if the Jewish people want to be accepted without undue reservation, they must assimilate without undue reservation. FUBU ("For Us By Us") a clothing line created by black Americans ostensibly for black Americans sends a mixed message. On one hand, it sends a message of solidarity and mutual aid from blacks to blacks. Looked at another way, especially in our world of affirmative action and political correctness, it sends a message of separation that some may perceive as alienation and defiance. No judgment here, just recognition of both sides of a particular social "coin" and an invitation to discuss our differences and similarities at the DayLight Forum.

King Cotton: The principal rationale for bringing slaves into this country was a desire for cheap labor; especially a need to harvest large fields of cotton on an economical basis. Can you imagine how different and better off the world would be if the cotton gin had been invented 100 years earlier? We need to ask ourselves if there is perhaps a similar technological, spiritual or political breakthrough on the horizon that can help unite us regardless of color, religion or political persuasion. Finding that kind of solution is at the very core of The DayLight Movement. Instead of focusing outward, and trying to force sovereign nations to conform to our way of life, we need to search for peace amongst ourselves.

> **"I do not believe in a fate that will fall on us no matter what we do. I do believe in a fate that will fall on us if we do nothing. ... Let us renew our determination, our courage, and our strength. And let us renew our faith and our hope."** *Ronald Reagan*

America's collective racial attitude extends far beyond its physical borders. It's about our willingness (or lack thereof) to help non-white people in foreign countries who are in desperate straits. It seems like, the darker their skin the less likely that America will get involved. Together, we will explore racial and religious bigotry, treatment of the American Indian, and virtually any other subject that our fellow DayLight Forum visitors wish to bring into the light of day. We will choose group leaders from amongst us who will lead individual issue-defined forums within the main Forum. You don't need to be an expert to participate or even lead one of these forums; you just have to care and show up.

"80% of success is showing up." *Woody Allen*

CHAPTER 16

HUMAN RIGHTS

"The care of human life and happiness, and not their destruction, is the first and only legitimate object of good government."
Thomas Jefferson

When I set about to convey your opinions about human rights, I thought this chapter would be one of the longest and most extensive of all. In the final analysis, it all boils down to a prime example of the adage, "The bigger the problem the simpler the solution." A simple rule, that anyone can follow, applies:

Treat everyone as if they were God in disguise. If you do not believe in God then pretend that they're capable of doing, only 10 times worse, what you are doing to them because history tells us that is what usually happens.

For those torturers and oppressors who appear to escape this life unpunished it seems far-fetched that the intelligence that created all of us would not have something in store for them.

In his second inaugural speech President Bush called for the United States to spread democracy throughout the world: "Only one force is strong enough to break through hatred and tyranny,' he said, 'and that is the force of human freedom." In the spring of 2006, even staunch supporters from his own Republican party were stepping back from his assertion. If we are to be a truly great superpower we must *advocate*, not force, the concept of freedom and human rights throughout the world.

"The key ingredient of Democracy is beyond holding elections and instituting majority rule, it is the safeguarding of the rights of the minority and maintaining the rule of law – the societal structure in which we can feel safe from unfair treatment." *Kevork Toroyan*

Organizations, like **Human Rights First** (www.humanrightsfirst.org) work throughout the world "to create a secure and humane world – advancing justice, human dignity, and respect for the rule of law. [They] support human rights activists who fight for basic freedoms and peaceful change at the local level; protect refugees in flight from persecution and repression; help build a strong international system of justice and accountability; and make sure human rights laws and principles are enforced in the United States and abroad." At times organizations, like this and the ACLU, may seem to be at odds with the national consensus on a particular matter, but their sincere attempts at helping all of us to do well by each other is certainly worth the any potential disagreement about how to proceed. Here, too, the DayLight Movement will provide a means for these organizations to clarify or expand their positions and educate us about their mission and goals for society.

CHAPTER 17

WOMEN

CRIMES AGAINST HUMANITY

"Be it in business or in the home, why do men abuse women? Because they think they can get away with it." *Anonymous*

Racism is not the only social crime that we must unite to intelligently address and stop. Crimes against women – physical and mental abuse; discrimination in schools and the workplace; lesser rights, legal standing, and pay than men simply for not being one; genital mutilation; criminal prosecution for consensual sex or, even worse, for being raped; must be dealt with in no uncertain terms. All are crimes against humanity.

"The majority of the 1.5 billion people living on 1 dollar a day or less are women.
Women constitute 75% of the poorest people in the world today.
Women produce half the world's food, but own only 1% of its farmland.
Two-thirds of illiterate adults are women."
CARE: a leading humanitarian organization fighting global poverty.

While it would be nice to say that, once we get our own American house in order, we can start to share our example with the rest of the world, the plain fact is that women are suffering and dying at such an incredible rate that we must press for change throughout the world NOW. We can start by setting a better example in the US; the details of which we will develop at the DayLight Forum.

If a nation is not protecting its women, the world must embargo it just as it would if that nation were caught committing any other offense worthy of embargo. How did human beings first decide that women were less than equal? At the dawn of time, it likely had to do with simply being the physically weaker sex. That might be understandable back in our cave-dwelling days but how is it that, in the 21st century, males continue to turn against and violate the very gender group who gave them life and with whom they bonded with their very first breath outside mother's womb?

Surely the frequent, worldwide, reports of rape, beating and killing of innocent, defenseless, women has penetrated our selfish societal veil to a degree where even the least aware of us realizes that this is a far greater problem than just the criminal acts themselves. There is an underlying *attitude* that we must address. The very evolution of the human species cannot progress until we have eradicated this societal and spiritual poison from the world's circulatory system. Granted, there will likely always be individual cases of gender-related crimes of insanity but even those will likely be reduced once we have removed the stench of sexual deviancy, cruelty and condescension from the air that we breathe. We must try.

ABORTION: "LADIES CHOICE"

One of the most hotly debated feminine and political topics is a woman's right to have an abortion. I chose to emphasize this subject over other equally troubling topics, like those touched upon above, because, as of this writing, the right to an abortion is under fire in South Dakota – a neocon-driven precursor to a fight that will ultimately tumble into the Supreme Court. That challenge highlights three primary points of contention:

- The majority of women feel abused by a legal system that they assert has no business intruding into their lives.
- Those who support the right to have an abortion consider a ban to be discriminatory and unrealistic because making it illegal will simply force low-income women to turn to back-alley abortionists while wealthier women can have the procedure performed in another country.
- Both sides of this issue consider the other side's position to be a crime of abuse.

Clearly, this subject calls for our input at the DayLight Forum as soon as possible.

I preface the conversation starters offered below with full acknowledgement that, because I am not a woman, I cannot truly know how someone feels at such a point in her life, and that nothing written here can resolve what should be a quintessential matter of conscience rather than law – a matter between a woman and her chosen advisors not legislators, most of whom do not even represent her state. What I can say with a high degree of certainty is that those on opposite sides of this issue will never agree, and that we can neither legislate morality nor define abortion in terms that will satisfy all of us. At best, the subject of abortion will continue to be batted back and forth through the courts until science creates a 100% reliable method of birth control that makes a woman infertile until she specifically chooses to conceive (at which point the Catholic Church will likely chime in), or until a scientific definition of the beginning of life is agreed; the latter being a virtual impossibility.

"Pro-choice or Pro-life," we can talk until we are "blue in the face" about how abortion should not be legislated but reality says that, for the kind of politicians that we currently elect, it is too hot of a political issue – too much of an opportunity to pander for votes – for them to ignore. In their defense, they have been forced into this position largely by the Religious Right, which never misses an opportunity to press its values on society. Taking charge of our nation via local, state, regional and national referendums will take the pressure off of our elected officials to pontificate and perform for a powerful religious lobby that can write bigger checks than can pregnant women who were raped; know that they have a highly defective fetus; or whose life is in danger. A new breed of "DayLight" politician/ombudsman will advise us rather than kowtow to a lobbying force that cannot possibly adjudicate every woman's situation and decision process.

By the way, can anyone show me where the Koran, the Torah or the Old or New Testament address abortion? Surely something this important would qualify for at least the same treatment as how an owner should treat his slaves. Offering up "Thou Shalt Not Kill" sounds reasonable, at first, until we get into specifics like, "Does this commandment apply to wasted sperm? An ovum? A zygote? One, two, ten or more cells? An entity without a formed brain?" Where do we draw the line about what threatens a mother's life?" What is the difference whether she bleeds to death giving birth or dies of depression or illness caused by the stress of having to raise a child alone or within an abusive marriage where the father clearly did not want the child from the day it was conceived?

In her blog entitled: *"A Religious Argument For Being Pro-Choice,"* (http://ever-increasing-entropy.blogspot.com/2006/02/religious-argument-for-being-pro.html) Caitlyn Martin writes:

"Exodus 21:22-23 rules that if two men are fighting and one murders the pregnant wife of the other, the killer is executed. But if instead of killing the wife, he wounds her and causes her pregnancy to be aborted, 'the assailant shall be fined.' As this passage makes clear, whatever value the fetus has, the Hebrew Bible (which Christians call the Old Testament) doesn't grant the status of human life.

In a nation where one of its chief founders, Thomas Jefferson, called for 'a wall of separation between church and state' imposing a ban on abortion based on one religious belief, no matter how prevalent, is simply wrong. If polls are right a majority of Americans are pro-choice in any case, not that numbers should matter. I, as a member of a religious minority, do not want to see any one religion or set of beliefs given supremacy over all others. That issue goes far beyond abortion. Once that happens, once the United States starts moving towards theocracy, it would no longer be a country I could be comfortable living in. Banning abortion based on Christian religious belief is, indeed, theocratic.

I certainly don't want the state or someone else's religion making medical decisions, which could have severe consequences for the woman involved for the rest of her life."

Ms. Martin's closing statement is especially salient in light of organized religion's propensity to modify its rules as society changes. I would hate to see someone imprisoned in this life, or think that they were damned to hell for something that may not be considered a sin a year after they pass on. I am well aware of the concept, "If you think it's a sin, it's a sin," but I also know that, due to immaturity, inexperience, or respect for tradition and their teachers, people often accept things that simply are not true or no longer apply.

The following statistical information was extracted from About.com's Women's Issues "Abortion Statistics" page, and the Alan Guttmacher Institute.

- In 54 countries (61% of the world population) abortions are legal.

- In 97 countries (39% of the world population) abortions are illegal.

- There are approximately 46 million abortions conducted each year, 20 million of them obtained illegally.

- There are approximately 126,000 abortions conducted each day.

- Approximately 1,370,000 abortions occur annually in the U.S. according to the Alan Guttmacher Institute

- 88% of abortions occur during the first 6 to 12 weeks of pregnancy [Day Light editorial note: at this stage a fetus is about 2 inches long and weighs less than an ounce. The great majority of neonatologists assert that no baby is viable before the 22nd week.].

- 60% of abortions are performed on women who already have one or more children.

- 47% of abortions are performed on women who have already had one or more abortions.

- 43% of women will have had at least one abortion by the time they are 45 years old (this statistic includes miscarriages in the term "abortion").

- The majority of women getting an abortion are young. 52% are younger than 25 years old and 19% are teenagers. The abortion rate is highest for those women aged 18 to 19 (56 per 1,000 in 1992.)

- 51% of women who are unmarried when they become pregnant will receive an abortion. Unmarried women are 6 times more likely than married women to have an abortion. 67% of abortions are for women who have never been married.
- 63% of abortion patients are white, however, black women are more than 3 times as likely to have an abortion, and Hispanic women are 2.5 times as likely.

- 43% of women getting an abortion claimed they were Protestant, while 27% claimed they were Catholic.

The idea of killing a live human being is beyond abhorrent but, for many, so is being forced to make a lifelong commitment for a 5-minute mistake, accident or rape. The pro-life answer is, "No matter what the circumstances of your pregnancy may be (excluding danger to the life of the mother), you need to have your baby and either raise it lovingly or give it to someone who will." Additionally, Pro-lifer's feel that a woman who chooses to terminate her pregnancy, or to complete it only to give her baby up for adoption, makes that choice because she does not want to be inconvenienced, publicly embarrassed or both. Pro-life asks, "How else can you explain the overwhelming urge to deny a primordial, primeval, nurturing instinct that is so firmly embedded in a woman's very DNA? Are we not capable of countering that urge with intellect and offsetting our inconvenience or shame when the alternative is killing a human being?"

Pro-choice refutes this, asserting that no one undergoes such a detailed procedure callously or without serious consideration. As one Pro-choice advocate put it, "Embarrassment or inconvenience doesn't begin to describe what these girls and women are feeling. Their emotions are much more likely to be fearful, feeling unable to support a child, and determined to not bring one into what is often a highly dysfunctional life situation that they do not believe can be resolved in time to make a life-long commitment that is suddenly staring them in the face – often alone."

Setting aside judgment about whether her decision is "good" or "bad," and assuming that giving birth will not endanger the life of the mother, what do we do in cases when we know that a fetus will be mentally or physically handicapped or in such perpetual and excruciating pain that it will be better off not living? Who decides? I submit that it is not a decision for men to make. Abortion does not affect a man's body nor does his DNA program drive him to accept the same high level of responsibility – typically an engagement of 18 or more years – like it does with a woman. Thus, women should be accorded this right to decide if for no other reason than because it is they who raise most of the children in this world. What do you think would be the vote if Congress were all-women?

NOT JUST "LADIES CHOICE?"

An often-overlooked aspect of the right-to-decide controversy is where does the father figure in? What are his rights? If two people engage in consensual sex and the woman becomes pregnant, what rights does the father have, especially if the woman was negligent or deceitful in her use, or purported use, of birth control? What if the father is willing to raise the child?

OPTIONS THAT A WOMAN AND SOCIETY CAN LIVE WITH

The vexing, oft-argued but never resolved, subject of abortion presents a prime opportunity to see what the *collective intelligence* of the DayLight Forum – you, me and those who will join us – can offer either from an ethical standpoint; by means of a massively difficult and long restructuring of society and how we live; or by developing a totally reliable form of birth control that makes the topic of abortion moot. In the meantime, we can take immediate action by creating a fund, that I would like to see us raise, which would go to supporting programs that will help an unmarried pregnant woman through her pregnancy, give her a place to live during her pregnancy if needed, and provide parental training and vocational or other training required for employment, and follow-up support whether she keeps or puts her child up for adoption. This brings to mind yet another reason why we need to stop spending literally hundreds of billions of dollars on needless wars and, instead, finance a study of these potential solutions and more as they arise. Trite as it may sound, if we can put a man on the moon, we should be able to solve this earthbound challenge, thereby saving the lives of literally millions of mothers and children.

Fair pay, discrimination in all forms, all forms of abuse, outmoded-to-ridiculous societal norms and religious customs that have no validity in civilized society, need to be dealt with equal fervor at the DayLight Forum. To those who care: come.

CHAPTER 18

CHILD ABUSE
THE "GIFT" THAT KEEPS ON GIVING

As a co-founder of a child abuse prevention center, and a trained mandated reporter, I have some experience with this subject. The path to America regaining its status as the greatest nation on earth must go through its children. To avoid suffering the same fate as those 19 of 22 civilizations, which, according to Arnold Toynbee's previously mentioned *A Study of History, "... collapsed when they reached the moral state America is in today,"* we must start with our children.

Abusing them mentally, physically and sexually robs them of the natural power of the human spirit – that little glimmer that we see in virtually every new baby's eyes. It is a law of human nature that, if you take away that power by force (beatings, rape, cruel words, even neglect), that little human will grow into a person who is focused on getting it back. The tragic part is the way that they attempt to get their power back is usually by the same means that it was taken. Beat your child and they will likely beat theirs. Abuse your spouse in front of a child and that child will do the same to their spouse and likely every member of the opposite sex with whom they come in contact. Hence a vicious generational cycle that gives true meaning to the term, "the gift that keeps on giving." What rolls forth is not a gift to society at all but rather a poison that attacks not just the carrier but all who come in contact with him or her.

Beatle, John Lennon, is reported to have suggested that Hitler might not have become such a societal monster if he'd just heard the word "love" and received more of it as a child. Common sense and any parent's experience tell us that John was right.

CHAPTER 19

GUN CONTROL

Six simple points:

1. While mandatory sentencing in general is a bad idea, mandatory sentencing for use of a deadly weapon is a good idea.
2. Commit a crime with a gun, and you get the death penalty or life in prison without the chance of parole.
3. Participate but not as a shooter in a premeditated crime, or be a driver in a fatal drive-by shooting, where someone other than you uses a gun, and get up to life in prison with the possibility of parole. If the shooting victim lives: 15 years to life-without-parole depending on the degree of permanent injury. If you are just a passenger, get out of the vehicle and walk home or face 1- 5 years as an accessory. This should make a lot of potential criminals "honorary crime fighters" and prompt them to choose their friends wisely.
4. Get caught with an unlicensed gun, first time 6 months, no early out. We will assume you have learned your lesson so, get caught again and go to prison for 1 year, no early out. Get caught again, or if you have prior felonies, go directly to jail for a minimum of 5 years. No early out.
5. Get caught in a vehicle with someone with an unlicensed gun: 30 days in jail (if we can enforce a seatbelt law, we can enforce this). This will recruit more self-policing "citizen deputies" to help dissuade gun crime; especially drive-by shootings.
6. If someone uses your gun in a crime and you cannot prove that it was stolen from a secure place, go to jail for a minimum of 1 year. No, we don't care if ruins your or your family's life. You obviously didn't care about what it did to the victim and their family.

CHAPTER 20

HOMOSEXUALITY

WE ARE ALL GOD'S CHILDREN

This chapter is a good place to remind you that the intention of this book is to provoke discussion, not to assert a particular opinion or comment as fact. Over the four-year course of research and writing *ResoNation* I found that, when I solicited opinions about the subject of homosexuality, people were far more candid one-on-one than in a group. One sentiment that was frequently expressed in both settings was "live and let live." The consensus was:

> "Whatever else you might say or think, homosexuals are God's children and our fellow citizens, brothers, sisters, sons and daughters. If what they do is wrong, then let God judge. We simply need to live and let live. We can try to show them "the right way" by example but, just as no one can show another how to believe in God, we must let the recipients of our message chose or decline to accept it."

The Bible calls homosexuality an "abomination." With regard to male homosexuality, shoving ones sex organ into the same canal from which one defecates certainly qualifies for that definition in the minds of most people; heterosexual or not. While it is certainly decried in numerous Bible passages, some argue that homosexuality is not specifically addressed in the Ten Commandments. Even it if was clearly identified on those tablets, we do not publicly discriminate against other sinners so, no matter how abhorrent homosexuality may be to most of us, we should not discriminate here, either. We do, however, demand that our gay fellow citizens respect our feelings and traditions as much as they want theirs to be respected. This applies in particular to heterosexual traditions like "marriage."

While no one absolutely knows the mind of our Creator, it seems probable that, if homosexuality is wrong, He will deal those who practice it, in due time – so we don't need to stick our noses into someone else's spiritual destiny. To many of us, He certainly seems to be following a discernible course. Our gay brothers and sisters can scream "political incorrectness" all they want but *common sense*, not *bigotry*, tells us that the origin and most typical method of distribution of the AIDS epidemic (and the consequences thereof) speaks to this issue loud and clear.

Attempts at "sanitizing" or making AIDS more "acceptable" by pointing out that needles or innocent blood transfusions can also transmit it, are intellectually, morally, and needlessly dishonest. Granted, there are two sides to the AIDS crisis: those who, by their reckless actions, bring it on themselves; and those who innocently contract it via a blood transfusion, rape, being born of an infected mother, or by accident (e.g. a needle stick by a nurse). Thus, AIDS is no longer just a homosexual malady. We've been bombarded by so many facts, figures and statistics that I won't foist them on you here. Instead, I will offer what is perhaps the only practical solution: *We must take care of each other.*

The world needs to stop wasting money on unnecessary wars and start spending it on education, research and treatment. We have heard this so many times and we have become so jaded that it isn't even registering anymore. I ask you to open your ears, mind and heart to this:

> The eradication of AIDS will never happen within the scope and capabilities of literally *any* form of government currently in existence because politicians are leery of being tagged pro-gay when they should be concerned solely with being pro-human. Only a referendum-based vote that is cast in the privacy of a voting booth or other voting venue will move this issue to a happy resolution; thereby relieving our elected officials from having to take an "uncomfortable" stand on either side of an issue that is more a matter of health and humanity than politics.

Marriage is yet another subject where "political correctness" has swung too far to the left of center. Homosexuals certainly deserve the right to a civil union between two people but, just as they insist on respect from the heterosexual community, they need to respect heterosexual feelings about a spiritual rite that was created by the heterosexual segment of society.

Calling same-sex unions "marriage" rests on "the lie of repetition:" Do something long enough and it becomes "right" in society. The majority of We-the-People believe in "live and let live and let God take care of the details" but, just because some of our fellow citizens do something long enough – something that has been repugnant to community standards for thousands of years – does not lend it "validity by virtue of longevity."

America was founded on certain principles. As we do with those immigrants who want to usurp our Christian foundation, I advise our gay fellow Americans to pick your battles carefully and not force a needless issue. I'm sure that your love for each other is as strong and sincere as heterosexual love and that both groups have just as many shallow, insincere, members. Your understandable desire to have your unions blessed is the same *desire for validation* that we all have. But you must face facts. Your "marriages" are not about creation. They are about simple cohabitation and personal gratification. That may be well and good but does it have to be made into a national debate? Call your spiritual link-ups "civil union" (with all the legal spousal entitlements) and get on with your life or face an unnecessary fight ad infinitum. Besides, in this turbulent world, we all have bigger fish to fry and we need to work together on so many other more pressing matters.

Just as Jewish Americans and black Americans need to assimilate (and be permitted to assimilate) more into society so, too, do homosexuals need to be sensitive to things that needlessly throw up barriers and keep us separate and wary of one another. A prime example is public display of affection ("PDA"). Gay or straight, a short buss or hug is not likely to offend your fellow citizen's sensibilities. The problem with overdone gay PDAs is that they bring to mind what a large part of society considers to be disgusting practices like the aforementioned anal penetration. That's not love or even caring sex. That's plain old selfish public gratification. You can shout, "Well, get over it!" all you want but that won't change the way most of your fellow Americans feel. About some things we all should have the good sense to stay private.

Before the "politically correct mafia" takes umbrage, I encourage them to consider "community decency standards;" a term that has been derisively attacked by a morally anarchic cast of characters (gay and straight) who advocate a vast array of hedonistic forms for gratifying the flesh. I may not like your practices and you may not like mine but let's try to keep what should be private behavior out of public view. We'll all get along much better that way.

PART THREE:
FOREIGN AFFAIRS

CHAPTER 21

WAR

There is more than one route to freedom, and each nation must find its own or fail to find it at all. Freedom cannot be imported, or imposed by decree. It can only be fostered in harmony with a society's own culture, character and circumstances.
Paul Greenberg

Unless our homeland is actually being attacked, the case for engaging in an offshore war is virtually impossible to support. Vietnam and Iraq are perfect examples. Young men and women are suckered into false patriotism, paid dirt wages, their families are destroyed, and then we wonder why we have low morale and trouble recruiting a strong army. We-the-People must take away the power of politicians to lie to these young men and women, and to us, about things like Vietnam and Iraq.

In the 1960s, our "experts" panicked us with their since-repudiated "domino theory" about how the loss of Vietnam would lead to all of Asia falling to communism at a time when communism could not even support itself. In short, we did not believe in ourselves and we did not believe that freedom and free enterprise were far superior. If we had believed, we would have known that communism is fundamentally flawed morally and economically. Sadly, our leaders knew the condition of the leading communist economies, but they did not tell us because they succumbed to the military-industrial complex's ravenous need for income that comes from war and the specter of war. Once again, Big Money and special interests won out.

In this respect, our current situation in Iraq is no different from Vietnam decades ago. We had no business invading Iraq and we have no business staying there. First it was because they had weapons of mass destruction ("WMDs"). When that specious ploy failed, it was because, "Saddam Hussein killed so many of his own people." While that is reprehensible, Hussein was not killing *our* people. Now our reckless and needless incursion has resulted in the death of over 2,700 American soldiers and the permanent, life-ruining, maiming of another 18,000.

"When will we ever learn? When will we ever learn?" *Pete Seeger*

When we could not find the WMDs that our President and our vaunted intelligence agencies touted, we changed the name of our incursion to "Project Iraqi Freedom." The truth is, we are not over there to liberate the Iraqi people or because We-the-People want to be there; we are there because it is profitable for the military-industrial complex's Big Money beneficiaries who finance our politicians' increasingly expensive election campaigns and because politicians on both sides of the aisle think that wars get people re-elected.

On March 17, 2004, CBS Radio quoted Henry Hyde, Representative of Illinois, as saying that Spain's decision to withdraw its troops from Iraq would be a "victory for al-Qaeda." Sorry, Congressman. Al-Qaeda scored its victory when the United States blundered into Iraq and gave the fanatics one more reason to die, and take as many people as possible with them. Now they have yet another "cause" to add to their litany of hatred for America. Did the Iraqi people attack us? How many of the September 11th hijackers were from Iraq? Reports say 15 of 19 were from Saudi Arabia.

What are we doing invading a sovereign nation and sacrificing American lives to fight someone else's battles – even worse, for people who hate us? What are our young military and civilian support men and women dying for? Will Iraq's new government be an ally of the United States, or will it just be a new set of fanatical, America-hating faces? If part of our mission was to intimidate the leaders of the other "Axis of Evil," rogue nations, could we not have accomplished this by simply taking out Saddam Hussein and his team? Like politicians throughout the world, aren't these rogue leaders as interested, if not more interested, in remaining in power as they are in their people's well being?

Are we stabilizing the Middle East? For the answer to that question look no further than to neighboring Israel's purposely-provocative "Gestapo" tactics (e.g., the 2002 Jenin massacre and related U.S.-aided cover-up; and the Berlin Wall-like Jerusalem border wall) that are going on while we distract the world with the unnecessary horror of an Iraqi occupation. Fanning the flames of Arab freedom fighters is not the way to win the peace; and we wonder why they immolate and behead Americans whenever they get the chance.

No one on either side of the Middle East's constant strife will trust America until we have a government that all can trust. America needs more than just a new foreign policy; we need a *direct means* of expressing our true values and desires about how our country should operate both internally and on the world stage. A good start will be to move to local and national referendums, and away from reliance on people who are more concerned with power than with the safety and welfare of those who empower them with their precious votes. When the fanatics who bomb trains in Spain see that we are earnestly trying to bring sanity to our domestic and foreign policy, perhaps they will, in turn, behave more sanely. What have we got to lose compared to the loss of human life, property and hard dollars wasted in a desert 6,000 miles away?

President Bush and company have piled on ridiculous rationale after rationale for pushing us into war and imposing ourselves in Iraq. In his January 21st, 2004 State of the Union address, Bush claimed that we invaded Iraq because "democracies don't breed terror." Hogwash; we are a democracy and we have been a prime breeder of terror ever since we and the British confiscated Palestinian land and gave it to their sworn enemies to form the new state of Israel. A centuries-old theocratic culture, infused with a high level of religious fervor, if not outright fanaticism, will ensure that any democracy that we try to *install* in the Middle East will soon fall and the cycle of death will start all over again.

Taking out Saddam was not the United State's unilateral responsibility; it was a job for the international community. The problem is that our standing at the UN and on the world stage is so poor, and of such a bullying nature, that we have far less influence than we could have. So, instead we started a war and have incurred, in present and future expense, $1 Trillion and wasted thousands of American lives on a no-win cause. If we truly felt that we had to take action on our own, we could have offered a $1 Billion bounty to any individual who brought Saddam Hussein and Osama bin Laden in, dead or alive, for their crimes against humanity and violations of international law. We could then have applied the $398 Billion balance to our education and healthcare systems, the elderly, and to paying our military service personnel a decent wage.

"If you kill the head, the body will follow:" Foreign tyrants' sins are not our business. The people of a troubled country must find a way to take out their corrupt, murderous leaders themselves. They do not need to surmount the tyrant's bodyguards, they just need to take out the tyrant – the daily terror bombings in Baghdad are certainly proving the efficacy of this tactic. If assassins and would-be-assassins could get to three leaders of the modern free world (President's Kennedy, Ford and Reagan) they certainly should be able to get to the Saddam Husseins of the world.

Doesn't it seem strange that the Bush team did not recruit Mossad, Israel's crack anti-terror unit and publicly recognized assassination squad, to take Saddam Hussein out? After all, we give Israel, in one form or another, more than $6 Billion per year (30% of our total foreign aid budget) for basically doing nothing other than being a "thorn in the Arab world's side." Do you really think that act would have endangered Israel any more than it is now? Can anyone "connect the dots" between the principal beneficiaries of the Iraq invasion, the military contractor Halliburton, and its former CEO, Richard Cheney?

The leaders of both political parties have failed to take care of the people who take care of us. What kind of leader, what kind of value system, what kind of country, spends billions of dollars on people who hate us, and at the expense of our grossly underpaid soldiers who put their lives on the line to defend us? This is a perfect example of why we need to take more control of our destiny and safety, rather than rely on elected officials to do what we all know is right. We need to act *now*, before more dollars and lives are needlessly lost. The 2008 election is looming. Considering the poor quality of a weak 2004 candidate field, now is a perfect time to start injecting DayLight into what has become a quadrennial mudslinging farce. Although we likely will not accomplish our goal of a full-on direct democracy system before the 2008 elections we can get a good start if we act now.

While it may seem far-fetched at first, perhaps we need to keep an open mind and "think outside the box" about what we can do to distract mankind from its aggressive, territorial proclivity for conflict. It has been suggested by some pundits that the only thing that could unite all of us would be "an attack from outer space." Perhaps we could take the initiative and "attack outer space" with a new, visionary program that can light up our imaginations like President Kennedy did with our "man on the moon" mission. In addition to rebuilding the hurricane-devastated Gulf Coast (this time in an environmentally sound way), let us seriously explore the idea of visiting Mars as a way to recharge our economy with new jobs and a vision beyond our ingrained religious and political hatreds. It is in man's very DNA to explore and extend our reach into the universe. The Vikings, Christopher Columbus, and even the Pilgrims did precisely that. Let us focus our time, passion, and money on something other than war. The military-industrial complex will still thrive; they will just have to build machines for peace, not for death. Dr. Matthias Rath put it well when he said, "War is not a sign of strength, it is a sign of desperation."

> **We must come to see that peace is not merely a distant goal we seek, but it is a means by which we arrive at that goal. We must pursue peaceful ends through peaceful means."**
> *Martin Luther King, Jr.*

CHAPTER 22

TERRORISM

The bombs are likely already here. We can't defuse all the bombs but we may be able to diffuse the bombers

A recent email exchange between one of our fellow citizens and myself presents a good place to start:

GregO:
Why are you pressing for us to get out of Iraq? I guess that you only see the issue from the side of the cowards - "run, coward, run." Run and they will take your lifestyle, your wife and your children and you will be slaves to a life you never thought possible.
Tim

Dear Tim:
You've got it all backward, my friend. It takes a coward to attack a little, virtually helpless paper tiger nation and a despot who was so toothless that he couldn't even fly over his own airspace. A nation that had no significant al Qaeda presence until the "madman triumvirate" of Bush, Cheney, and Rumsfeld played right into Osama bin Laden's hands. Thanks to them and their lies, Iraq is now rife with al Qaeda and drug cartel members. It would have taken a **real** *hero and statesman not to succumb to such a ploy.*

With respect to your assertion - "Run and they will take your lifestyle, your wife and your children and you will be slaves to a life you never thought possible" - just wait until they detonate a dirty bomb and put a major city out of commission for 15,000 radioactive half-life years. We need to assume that the bombs are already here. We cannot defuse the bombs, only the bombers. We need to engage their leaders in active, positive dialogue. The world and warfare have changed. It's city guerrilla warfare now. Instead of chasing down and killing Osama bin Laden, we need to bring him to a conference table. Killing him and his followers will only cause them to be replaced. It would be like stomping out ants: as fast as you kill them a message gets back to the nest and they step up reproduction.

I know you have good intentions. Consider doing some real good by praying for America and not advocating outdated diplomacy and war tactics.
GregO

Filmed news reports of our military hunting al Qaeda members in Afghanistan and Iraq give a powerful (but false) impression that we are actually doing something to combat terror. Let us not forget that it was not an al Qaeda army that attacked us on September 11th. A handful of U.S. pilot-trained thugs conducted that deadly affront. I supported our activities in Afghanistan, but only if we could catch the bad guys within the Bush Administration's initial estimate of 6 months. An extended campaign to catch someone who will only be quickly replaced by a compatriot with an equivalent mindset is a waste of lives, money and our international reputation. We have no business chasing people in countries that are not physical threats to us, and for reasons that will not make us any safer.

Like my friend, Tim, our current government has it all backward. As described later in this chapter, the solution to the terror crisis consists of a number of interlocking finite parts. Whether we are talking about Iraq, Iran or Syria, no matter who opens their inspection doors, to us or to the UN, we can never hope to reliably find all of a country's illicit items; especially weapons of mass destruction. We need to change our foreign policy and practice "diplomatic jujitsu" to take the pressure off all sides. We need to stop being cowed by the Jewish electoral lobby and help Israel to bring Palestine into the world community as an equal – a brother nation. We need to pull completely out of Iraq. If Iraq, or any country, gets taken over by an extremist Islamic group, we can embargo them from the rest of the world or let their fellow citizens take their bad guys out at a cost far less than what we have already paid at home, in Iraq, and in Afghanistan.

We also need a bolder World Court that will try despots in absentia, if need be, and put out "Wanted Dead or Alive" notices that, unlike the posturing of George W. Bush, really mean what they say; or we can put out the posters ourselves. At a Billion dollars per despot, we could rid the world of most its bad guys for less than what it costs to occupy Iraq for six months;

and at no loss of life. I can assure you that we would have far more truly committed allies on that mission than we have today. To those who argue that such an action would be too much like vigilantism to be acceptable in the court of world opinion, I ask, "could it be any worse than what we are currently doing?" To those who say that we cannot pull out because we will suffer a loss of face, I ask, "how much worse could our international reputation be?" Do we look stronger, or weaker in the eyes of "bad guys" who know we are spreading ourselves too thin globally and depleting even our great financial resources?

HOW TO DEFEAT INTERNATIONAL TROUBLEMAKERS

Pulling out of Iraq does not mean that we have to stop combating terror and the people who deliver it. Here in three simple steps is a strategy for combating terrorism and restoring order throughout the world:

I. **Recognize that terrorism can only work with popular support. Isolate the fanatics.** Win the hearts and minds of the people. How could supposedly the most brilliant and powerful military in the world blow it so badly in Iraq, yet get it so right in Afghanistan and Yemen? In Iraq, we fired the army and most of the civil servants and then compounded that egregious error by bringing in hired foreign private security personnel, and Halliburton employees to perform day labor work that could have permitted Iraqi civilians to earn money and maintain self-esteem. Does anyone still think that the security threat they *might* have posed could have been any worse than the one that has resulted in the death of 2,700 of our soldiers and ten times that many innocent Iraqi civilians?

II. **Use local intelligence.** Any army private knows that military and political intelligence is the most important thing in battle. When we arbitrarily fired the Iraqi army, and more importantly effected a whole sale firing of the internal security organizations (especially the Baath party security group), we lost the proverbial "local" who knows all the cultural "ins & outs" of a country and can get you anything or anyone. We couldn't even speak the language!

III. **Quietly advise, don't bully, don't stand out.** In Yemen, we don't embarrass the government by being too public with our presence. We don't fight; we advise and support. In Afghanistan, we let the local Northern Alliance clean up the country. Most of the world admires our values as expressed in our U.S. Constitution but they do not respect us as a people and often are against us, *because our policies do not reflect our stated values.* Al Qaeda's biggest enemy are the Middle Eastern governments that it wants to topple; especially the Royal Saudi family. Thus, perhaps more than anyone, Arab countries want to get rid of Middle East troublemakers but, for political and cultural reasons, they will not support America's overbearing involvement even when we claim we are fighting their battles. With the public mood in these countries being against us, primarily because of the Iraq war, these governments cannot be perceived to be helping the US. Iraq's neighbors fear the war spilling into their country and would have to step in to stop the fighting, as they did during Lebanon's civil war. Threatened gulf rulers will gladly bankroll an Arab army, led under UN pan-Arab regional auspices, to intervene in Iraq, not as a help to the US but to replace the US presence, which is perceived as an unwarranted and unwanted *occupation.* We do not need to unilaterally stage big military operations any more; we need to join the international club and co-operate with the rest of the world, not stand above it like an imperial taskmaster.

NOMAD NATION

The financial cost of Hurricane Katrina, and the fact that the Louisiana National Guard was not available to do its job because they were in Iraq, shows just how thinly stretched we are. The confusion, chaos, and traffic jams that resulted from hurricane-related evacuations in the late summer/early fall of 2005 will seem minor compared to having to permanently evacuate entire cities after a "dirty bomb" detonation. Bomb terrorists could actually drive the citizens of the most powerful nation on earth, like cattle, on a perpetual march. I fervently pray that we will come to our senses and change our foreign policy before such a national tragedy actually occurs.

Speaking of depleting financial resources, we need to take a serious look at whether we should be spending billions of dollars on overseas anti-terrorism programs such as the one recently proposed for the Philippines in order to prop up a leader who is vilified by her own people as corrupt and dangerous.

Virtually all experts, political and strategic alike, agree that we will continue to be vulnerable. There are Christians and Jews in places like New Zealand, yet no one is bombing or terrorizing that nation. Why not? Because New Zealand does nothing to anger terrorists. The way to truly combat terrorism is to stop calling their causes irrational (although their actions often are) and start listening and solving.

To my fellow Americans who live in the interior of our country: Do not think that you are safe. If New York City is completely compromised – not blown up, but simply poisoned by radiation for the next 15,000 years – the financial ramifications could put all of us in a dark hole for a very long time. And do not think that it will stop there. Dedicated terror cells have the luxury of time, obscurity, and surprise. Our cities can be taken down, one at a time. Neither embracing nor surrendering, We-the-People must engage in active and honest dialogue with the people who have this capability. That will not happen with our current form of government and its penchant for political posturing in a never-ending chase for votes. Until we change our foreign policy, we are no longer safe in our own beds.

MAKING US SAFE AT HOME

We need to face the fact that, even if the entire country embraced the Day-Light referendum model of government tomorrow, the currently entrenched Congress could stall such a transfer of power for years to come. This does not mean that we should not try to agitate for positive change; it just means that we must be realistic about doing other things in the interim that can help stop the vicious cycle of returning evil for evil. Here are just four of many anti-terror actions that are doable now. We owe it to future generations to start immediately.

First, we need to know who everybody is. The most effective way to accomplish that is to tie the privilege of driving, working, or receiving anything more than emergency government aid, to proof of identity and citizenship. President Bush and Congress found $1 Trillion (with more to come) to pay for a witch hunt invasion of Iraq and Afghanistan but, according to the *NumbersUSA Education and Research Foundation*, Congress could not come up with one tenth of that amount to help states standardize driver's licenses; an action that would be far more likely to protect us from terrorists than invading a weak paper tiger like Saddam's Iraq. Certainly in this day and age of computerization we can keep track of whom we let in and have the means to alert us when they have overstayed their welcome or committed an offense that disqualifies them from remaining here. If those who say that this would be logistically impossible are correct, then we must dramatically cut back the flow of visitors to a manageable level until we get our system straight.

Second, we must let the world know that Israel is here to stay, and that it is a demilitarized zone for all inhabitants and visitors – no weapons of any kind, other than for a UN peacekeeping force. While we are at it, why not a *nuclear free Middle East*, including Israel, plus a guarantee not to attack Iran or any other Middle Eastern country or try change their regime, if they will abandon their unilateral nuclear program and support of undesirable organizations that promote terror in such a demilitarized environment? Israelis and American Jews can greatly contribute to this effort by doing the kinds of things that I have described in the chapter on Israel.

Third, as most of the world already does, the U.S. must acknowledge that the decades-long depiction of the Palestinian fight for what is theirs' as "terrorism" must come to an end. These displaced Arabs are thinking, flesh-and-blood human beings, just like us. They are angry, not crazy. In fact, they are proving to be master strategists. Their cunning use of guerrilla tactics around the globe is stretching our military's defense capability and neutralizing our usual advantage of overwhelming force; "shock & awe" has lost much of its cachet. Even our own generals have admitted that we are stretched too thin. One of the most disconcerting storm clouds on the horizon is the fact that our troops are being called on to return too quickly to war zones for repeat tours. The result: dramatically lower rates of military enlistment and reenlistment. Soldiers are leaving in droves and our enemies are slowly bleeding our military to death. Our government's solution? Focus on recruiting minorities. Great, another war where we send a disproportionate number of our minority fellow Americans to fight and die for a nation that refuses to treat them as equals and to take care of them and their families while they are away and when they return.

Do you really think that minorities have some kind of extra "patriotism" gene or "war" gene that makes them want to enter the military in greater proportionate numbers than their Caucasian counterparts?

Or could it be a result of our failure to provide equal educational and job opportunities, a realistic minimum wage, and have shipped entry-level jobs overseas without any compensating offset? It seems that the old adage, "What this country's economy needs is a good war" is once again in vogue with a leadership that is clueless about how to solve our employment and poverty mess.

Fourth, parallel to these initiatives, we must do everything we can to engage our enemies in active dialogue. Traditional rules of war no longer apply. Negotiating with the enemy in an intelligent manner is not a sin if it stops them from killing us. We need to get off our high horse. This isn't like WWII, Korea or Vietnam where the oceans and our military might kept us safe at home. Our enemies have proven that they can get to us on our own soil.

The DayLight Forum presents a great venue to initiate sincere negotiation. We must, all of us, *"seek first to understand, then to be understood."* To those who say that we should never negotiate: we can go on being self-righteously indignant, or we can engage with people like Osama bin Laden in a peace-oriented dialogue. If we could engage General Tojo and his Emperor about Pearl Harbor, we should be able to establish a dialogue with the bin Ladens of the world, at least long enough to find a common ground that will defuse terror on a global scale. The alternative is to do what we have been doing. Bush's Secretary of State, Condoleeza Rice, "madly rearranging deck chairs on the Titanic" over in the Middle East, Europe and Africa looks and sounds good but is getting us nowhere. She and her initiatives are a "joke" to the Europeans and the Arab world. Macho utterances, such as those that President Bush likes to make from the safety of his Oval Office ("Bring it on!" and "Bring him in, dead or alive!"), must stop before we lose another thousand soldiers.

We may not like to negotiate with the enemy, but the practicality of life in the 21st century says that we must if we ever hope to bring a sense of peace and safety back into the world. This does not mean that we "roll over and play dead" or "give in." We-the-People will simply send a message to the world that we are willing to do everything that is fair and possible, and not one bit more. This message will ResoNate throughout the world and effectively neutralize the other side's international standing.

In the interest of fostering greater understanding of the challenge before us, perhaps the greatest obstacle to forcing democracy on Middle Eastern countries is their **religion-based refusal to cede authority** over their people, and our government's inexplicable failure to recognize this basic tenet.

> From *"The Independent,"* London, April 16, 2004:
> "Our own long history of colonial occupation has taught our army that there is a Newtonian law of military force. The application of military force by an occupier tends to produce an equal and opposite resistance by the occupied. That is why Osama bin Laden must be regarding events in Fallujah and Najaf with glee. What he wanted to achieve by demolishing the Twin Towers was confrontation between the West and the Arab world, and that is what George Bush has delivered in Iraq. And now he has delivered it in the Middle East too."

We cannot be a world leader by shoving our culture, our values, and our form of democracy down other nations' throats. We must lead by taking care of the sick, the ill, and the uneducated of the world. Unfortunately Big Money has other plans. It prefers to keep the world illiterate so as to perpetuate its ability to pay slave wages for cheap products that they can sell at Western prices. This misguided foreign policy invariably results in a loss of jobs at home and also the feeling, on the part of the "have-nots," of being abused by "the Great White Satan." Change our foreign policy paradigm and we will neutralize most, if not all, of those who are beating an ever-louder drum for our destruction.

If we truly want to bring democracy to the world, we need to *lead* it in, not force it in. Whether you are talking about Americans or citizens of other nations, no one can be led unless they agree to be led. Leadership and respect must be earned by spending time, money, and manpower on things that markedly improve people's lives, not on things that destroy their infrastructure in the name of installing democracy. This is the only way to change our current image from that of super-bully to true superpower. Today, most of the world perceives America as a nation displaying unbelievable greed fueled by a military-industrial complex mentality that defies common sense as it turns its back on morality in an unending quest for oil, money, and power. If our mission was truly to liberate oppressed people like the Iraqis, then why has Bush & Co. not invaded Africa? The answer is that there is not enough oil and the majority of the people who we would be helping have black skin.

PATRIOT OR TERRORIST?

Our government's propaganda program likes to classify anyone who violently disagrees with us, or with one of our favored special interest groups, as a "terrorist." King George of England felt the same way about our Revolutionary War heroes. However, in the eyes of much of the Christian and non-Christian world, these "terrorists" are viewed as patriots fighting against invading oppressors. Most of the world, including many of our allies in the West, separates the people who we call terrorists into two distinct groups: "fanatics" and "patriots." While it may sometimes seem difficult to discern which is which, a good rule-of-thumb to follow is to ask what they are fighting for:

> **If it is to force their religion or ideology onto others, they are fanatics and terrorists. If they are trying to retrieve property, freedom, or rights that were unlawfully taken from them, if they are fighting against someone else's culture and values being imposed on them, then they are "defenders" or "patriots."**

It really is as simple as that. Yasser Arafat was no more or less a terrorist than former Israeli Prime Minister Menachem Begin and his Irgun Zvei Leumi crew who went to prison for terrorist acts including a deadly bombing of the King David Hotel in 1946. Thus, when the term "terrorist" is used from this point forward, it will be in quotes to remind us to consider the difference between one man's "terrorist" and another's "patriot." This is not meant to condone violent action; only to help us understand why it is occurring. Although it may be convenient to associate "Evil" with "terrorism" we need to keep in mind that there are two sides to every story. One man's evil is another's necessity or last resort. One nation's penchant for "spreading democracy" is another's feeling of being invaded and bullied.

It is ironic that we call a major aspect of our new terror shield the "Patriot Act," for we brought the need for such an act upon ourselves when we created a new class of Arab patriot by forcibly evicting them from their land and giving it to their sworn enemies. Did America and the British really think that no one would fight for their home and their right to life, liberty, and the pursuit of happiness?

We have no business invading sovereign nations for the purpose of forcing democracy on them. Countries are not attacking us; individual *"terrorists"* who want us to leave their country and region alone are attacking us. Even Saddam Hussein would not have attacked us directly. Nor would he have been even covertly involved in such attacks because he knew that the world community would take him down – something that he thought (incorrectly) they would never permit the U.S. to do on its own. After being let off the hook by America and the senior Bush, Saddam never dreamed that we would actually invade over unproven allegations of WMDs. Even if these purported weapons had truly been secreted into Syria, invading Iraq was not the answer to stopping terrorism. If we believed they were in Syria, why didn't we invade Syria? Why hasn't the United Nations sent inspectors into Syria? Who is in charge?

Even the Atlantic and Pacific oceans are no longer barriers to people who want to kill us. The blood of fanaticism caused by our misplaced foreign policy is washing up on our shore, and We-the-People are the only ones who can staunch its flow. Toothless solutions like the Patriot Act will not stop determined fanatics, but they will do irreparable harm to our Constitutional rights. In addition to revamping our foreign policy, we need an information and intelligence gathering resource that works: one that could have told us as far back as the 1970s that Russia was not a superpower, but rather a crumbling, morally and financially bankrupt society on the verge of collapse; one that would have ensured that We-the-People were warned about reports of *impending attacks using public airliners*, rather than letting the "experts" decide to ignore, and later deny, the existence of such a report. Why didn't we know? Do you really believe it was bad intelligence or was it simply more of the same refusal to see the truth behind the lies that got us into Iraq?

The President's daily briefing memo of August 6, 2001, entitled *"Bin Laden Determined to Attack Inside the United States,"* specifically mentioned attacks using airliners, and yet We-the-People were taken completely by surprise. It is terrifying to think that, when evidence of this report was brought to light in the course of the 2004 election, the incumbent administration swept it into its long-running mix of lies and negative propaganda, thereby blinding most of us to the truth. I do not know which was worse, the lies or the fact that so many of us believed them.

While foreign and domestic intelligence gathering is critically important, we need to stop relying on the "magical powers" and prowess of the CIA and other "spook" agencies until we know that they are clean and not influenced by political pressure from Big Money and special interest groups. Consider the Bush administration's practice of twisting the facts presented in intelligence reports that said there were no WMDs in Iraq. Consider the **"Downing Street Memo"** in which, prior to the U.S. invasion, British Foreign Secretary Jack Straw opined, "If 11 September had not happened, it is doubtful that the U.S. would now be considering military action against Iraq. In addition, there has been no credible evidence to link Iraq with OBL (Osama bin Laden) and al-Qaida." Worried British officials warned Prime Minister Tony Blair that they feared the White House was rushing to an illegal war that never should have happened. And people wonder why much of the world calls Mr. Blair "Bush's lap dog."

We-the-People need to ensure that the heads of our intelligence agencies are thoroughly researched, and appointed by us based on recommendations from our elected ombudsmen, not by a man who disgraced the Presidential Medal of Freedom by presenting it to former CIA Director, George Tenet, an intelligence dilettante who was "asleep at the switch" when 9/11 hit.

The fact that our two major federal investigative and intelligence gathering agencies – the FBI and the CIA – were unable and, in most instances unwilling, to share information, highlights just how poor our leadership at the highest level of government has been; and probably for decades. The very definition of "intelligence" i.e., "the ability to comprehend, *cross-reference* and apply information" – the kind that could have precluded the attacks of September 11th – was ignored.

We need an intelligence system and a national leadership that saves a good man like Colin Powell from feeling the need to "toe the party line" by asserting that Iraq had weapons of mass destruction, and to remain relatively silent about the Bush Administration's initial estimate of the Iraq war's cost ("$50 Billion") and duration ("3-6 months"). He forgot that he owed his loyalty to the *American people*, not to someone who he knew was not telling the truth. As a former Chairman of the Joint Chiefs of Staff of the Armed Forces, he knew better yet, in one stroke, he compromised his credibility and political viability – perhaps forever. I say "perhaps" because the American public has a very short memory, which is one of our nation's greatest flaws. It is what lets the George W. Bush's of this world, and the operatives who they hide behind, get away with telling major-league lies. In our five-second-sound-byte, pressedfor-time society, the damning evidence underlying these lies fades quickly, leaving hardly a trace for the public's collective intellect to scrutinize. Luckily, bloggers are now helping to shine a bright light on the bad guys. Certainly, in this sense at least, they will be true allies of The DayLight Movement.

WHERE TO START

In addition to the steps offered earlier, one of the simplest and most effective means to reduce the threat of terror in our country is to simply stop sticking our nose in other people's affairs and, as mentioned earlier, trying to shove our values down their throats in the name of "spreading democracy." Our immoral and illegal eviction of law-abiding Palestinian Arabs in 1948 should have taught us that we cannot treat people like ignorant savages, ignore their cries for justice, and then expect them not to act out. So let's "cut to the chase" and address the most immediate terror challenge and its root: the global anger of Arabs (both Muslim and Christian), and most of the non-Arab world, over the United States' demonstrable favoritism of Zionist Israel to the detriment of its Arab neighbors.

Needlessly reckless acts like that 1948 eviction and now the invasion of Iraq provide current day "terrorists" with a heightened degree of credibility and fundraising power in the eyes of people, throughout the world, who see the wrong that was done and want to help do something about it. We can neutralize much of this by entering into a dialogue with the "terrorists," thereby putting them on the spot to put up or shut up – *"either specify your complaints so we can respond or go away forever."* This does not mean that we condone their actions or that we will sell out Israel. Although the way the State of Israel was formed was both illegal and immoral, we must face the fact that it exists, that it is not going anywhere, and that it can be made into a place of peace and prosperity to the benefit of Jew and Arab alike.

In light of our current leader's repeated failure to heed history and to stay out of war, We-the-People need to send a clear message to the world that we are actively working to create a new democracy in our own land – one that will once again make America a respected nation rather than a feared bully and inciter of terror. This just might buy us some time with the "terrorists" so that we can work with all parties on a consensus solution. If we do not, then more people than all of those killed in the Nazi Holocaust and Stalinist Russia will likely die in the coming years, if not months. Hyperbolic? Perhaps, but, in light of September 11th and the train bombings in London and Spain, who among us is willing to take that bet? Cling to the status quo, cling to material things, including ill-gotten Palestinian land, and we all will pay. Nothing permanent will change until the U.S. and Britain undo their wrong and start treating the Palestinians not as refugees but as equals to the people who were given their land and homes virtually overnight. Even respected military and political strategists are coming out in agreement with this.

During the February 9th 2005 edition of the *News Hour with Jim Lehrer*, retired General Michael DeLong and General Joseph Hoar (commander-in-chief of central command for U.S. forces in Iraq from 1991 to 1994) were interviewed. During the interview, General DeLong said, "every time I go over there [to the Middle East] in the past ten years, I get a finger pointed in my chest saying if you fix the issues between the Palestinians and the Israelis, there will be no terrorism in the world." General Hoar added to this: "It is the leitmotif that you hear every place you go in the Arab world that… 'we always support the Israelis at the expense of the Palestinians.' I have said again and again that the road to stability in Baghdad leads through Jerusalem."

These generals are not the only ones saying such things; the worldwide consensus is that September 11th would not have occurred, nor would the deaths of thousands of American soldiers, Iraqi civilians, Palestinians and Jews occurred, nor would $1 Trillion have been wasted, if we had handled the creation of an Israeli state in a decent and humane manner. Instead, reminiscent of what we did to the American Indians, we treated the Palestinians abominably, and then compounded our sin by persisting in that mindset for 58 years; and when they fight back, we have the gall to call them "terrorists."

This farce calls to mind a simple childhood analogy. A kid enlists the neighborhood cop on his beat to help him steal your bicycle. When you try to retrieve it, the cop calls you a troublemaker and puts you in jail. Then a judge who needs the thief's family's vote lets you out on the condition that you promise to behave while the perpetrator rides circles around you every day for the rest of your life. Only this isn't just about a bicycle. It's about literally waking up one day and looking through a barbed wire fence as your sworn enemy lives in your home and eats from your garden. How does someone get past that constant reminder? They don't. How do they grow as a person or nation? They don't. They just live with a hatred that soon extends well beyond the original beneficiaries and the people who aided them; eventually encompassing the abettor's innocent friends, neighbors and relatives.

$64,000 QUESTION

Answer this question: If someone credible had been able to warn us that the taking of Palestinian land to form Israel in 1948 would result in all of the suffering and bloodshed leading up to and including September 11th, and that it all could be averted if we just treat the Palestinians as well as the Jews, what would you have advised the U.S. and British governments to do?

The consequence of our failure to do the right thing is a widespread hatred of Jews just for being Jewish, not to mention a massive loss of life and financial resources all in the name of politics and pandering to Jewish electoral power. After being persecuted and hated by so many cultures and nations for 4,000 years, you would think that the Jewish leaders, and their American and British hatchet men, would have been more sensitive to the suffering incurred by displaced Palestinians. Instead, a half-century of needlessly callous disregard has brewed a resentment and hatred for Jews and Americans alike that has resulted in events like September 11th.

One would think that the first hundred or so suicide bombings in Israel would have prompted the oppressors to bring parity to the Palestinian side of the equation. Giving the evictees a decent place to live and real financial support over the past 58 years, not a piddling one tenth of the $6 Billion that we give to the Israelis annually, would have cost far less than the $1 Trillion price tag of war and wasted human lives in Afghanistan and Iraq. But the votes and power of Special Interest Groups operating under the cover of a nonsensical American Electoral College system blinded our politicians to what is right and what is wrong. The fact that all of this was transpiring 6,000 miles and a wide ocean away kept most of us asleep until the loudest alarm in history went off on September 11th. Our response? More invasion and more killing, which breeds more hatred and anger against us – not just from the Muslim world but also from some of our staunchest Western allies.

The Zion-obsessed Jewish political lobby would do well by its people to drop its mantle of hatred and condescending superiority and, instead, support fair treatment for the people who they so masterfully evicted. The charade that the eviction of 1948 was legal has gone on for so long that it has become "right" in the eyes of those who are too young to know what really happened; including many members of Congress. Adding to this blatant hypocrisy, we now want to force Syria to leave Lebanon while we occupy Iraq and Israel. Do any of us really think this will sit well with a culture where saving face is of paramount importance? Get ready for more blood to wash up on our shores.

Fanatics on both sides will ensure that the on-again-off-again Israeli-Palestinian series of peace initiatives will last only as long as the current leaders remain in power. Divorce yourself for a moment from the fact that a particular religion or people are involved. Anyone – Christian, Muslim, Jew, or any nationality – that had been so cruelly displaced would have fought back. Then, with clear eyes 58 years later, tell me if the situation is any better today. While it may be impossible to "put the toothpaste back in the tube" vis-à-vis the eviction of 1948, we must use our intelligence to explore and act upon every other reasonable solution. Bottom line: Israel has the potential to help bring peace to the world, but only if it's leaders stop egging on violence as a means to ensure that the United States continues to pay huge sums to "protect" it.

In late 2001, the following message was posted at www.AsimplePeace.org – a Website forum that some friends of many ideologies and faiths and I created. The proposal below was offered to President Bush in early 2002 and politely brushed off in a form letter from the White House. As this was written before Yasser Arafat's death, references to him will now apply to whomever currently occupies his position (currently Hamas Prime Minister Ismail Haniyeh) as leader of the Palestinian people. As you read the statement below, when you get to the point where it discusses making Iraq part of the Middle East peacekeeping force, think about what might have been:

> "Mankind can no longer ignore the fact that, the Israeli–Palestinian conflict is having drastic repercussions throughout the world. Many believe this conflict to be the root cause of the global radical Islamic terrorist movement and that, stopping it will cause radical factions throughout the world to at least pause their current global campaign. Every act of violence and inhumanity triggers, sometimes exponentially, evermore-violent responses by both fanatics and rational partisans alike whose causes, in some instances, may actually be noble but whose acts are horribly destructive.
>
> A 54-year cycle of Israeli-Palestinian peace talks followed by horrific fighting, followed by more peace talks and other "peace initiatives," followed by more violence has resulted in total failure. As evidenced by the September 11th tragedy, the blood of radical fanaticism on

both sides has overflowed the Middle East and is now washing up on the shores of Europe, Asia and the United States.

It is time for those who have a vested interest in sustaining the current state of chaos and violence to stand aside so that the truth can be dragged out into the light of day and peace and prosperity can once again be the right of all who are willing to work for it. ASimplePeace, via its 6-point Plan, is dedicated to ensuring that this happens. With your help, we can bring civilization back to the "cradle of civilization."

It is time for the world to face facts. Control of the violence in Israel is out of the Palestinian leadership's hands. Yasir Arafat can no more stop the suicide bombings than can the Israeli army, even if it is backed by all the armies in the world. This is a "moral" war being fought by people who, right or wrong and regardless of what their elected leaders may say, will continue to fight until their land is returned.

The understandably sympathetic response to the torture and mass murder of 6 million Jews caused the world to overcompensate by taking someone else's property for the purpose of giving Holocaust survivors a safe place to live. Many Jewish friends of ASimplePeace have reported that being "Israeli" and being "Jewish" are two different things. Those who have visited Israel in the past year (pre and post-September 11th) say uniformly that "the Israeli army is a bully and, at times, acts like Nazis." That's why over 1,200 soldiers (enlisted and officers) are now refusing to serve in the West Bank and Gaza. The international press reports that Israeli soldiers are harassing people, and doing despicable acts like driving tanks through narrow residential alleys, purposely destroying the walls of innocent people's homes on either side.

With all due respect for Mecca and the Vatican, for purposes of this discussion Jerusalem is the religious "center of the universe." It is also the center/focal point of the terror universe. This ancient city has been called the "nuclear engine" of a radical religious-fanatic terror movement that is fueled by perceived Israeli mistreatment of Palestinians, and the perception that America has taken the side of the Jews, unconditionally.

The Israelis have proven incapable of controlling an often brutal military that is largely funded by the United States. Israeli political leaders sustain themselves by constantly stirring up trouble at the expense of innocent (and some not-so-innocent) Palestinians because it gets votes. They have little incentive to reduce Middle Eastern tensions for fear that it will trigger a reduction of the $3 Billion that the United States government sends each year. Money that is used to buy the Jewish-American vote while providing a secure Middle Eastern haven for U.S. interests and a staging area for the U.S. and its allies in time of war or when the area's oilfields are threatened.

For proof of this assertion of a "constant troubles" dynamic tension mindset, one need look no further than Ariel Sharon's provocative visit (September 28, 2000), accompanied by heavily armed guards, to the top (i.e., the Islamic section) of the holy Temple Mount at a time of intense social unrest. Even members of the Israeli press argued that Mr. Sharon knew it would cause trouble, and that he views it as his job to "keep the pot boiling." Acts like this come from the same arrogant, hubristic mindset that claims that, because the land purportedly belonged to the Jews (who wrote the Old Testament) 2,000 years ago, it should have been given back to them even if others have called it "home" for centuries. ASimplePeace sympathizes with their yearning for a homeland, but maintains that neither religion nor religious history should ever be used as an excuse to take someone else's property.

Similar instances of provocative behavior by PLO leader Yasser Arafat and his lieutenants occur with alarming frequency. The difference is that Mr. Sharon & company are fighting to keep property that was taken from the Palestinians, and Mr. Arafat is fighting to get it back. His mission is noble, his tactics are not.

Trite as it may sound at first, "Love" is the answer to both the Israeli-Palestinian crisis and the larger problem of sectarian violence that plagues the entire world. When two unruly toddlers violently squabble over a prized possession, a responsible parent separates them and, if mediation fails, he or she "lays down the law" with love, not hate or retribution favoring one over the other. The fact that the U.S. and Britain forcibly formed the country of Israel and that the U.S. alone sends over $6 Billion to Israel annually constitutes "parenthood."

It is time for America and the UN to take the "high ground" by stepping in and separating the Palestinian and Israeli combatants by the scruffs of their necks and then laying down rules of conduct from that point forward. Only then can cooler heads prevail. This is far better than continuing to let them kill one another, and giving radical fanatics a rationale and a platform to kill not only Americans, but citizens of virtually every nationality and religion like they did on September 11th. The Holy Land belongs to the world, not to either side in this dispute.

The solution to the root cause of what happened on September 11th, and to the devastating violence in Israel and Palestine, can be summed up in six points:

1. The United Nations – and the United States and Britain specifically – must take responsibility for its 1948 mistake, no matter how well intended it may have been. Three of the most courageous words in any language are: "We were wrong." This simple statement can help to melt the hatred, sadness and resentment that have grown like a cancer inside millions of people for over 50 years. "Peace" will then obediently follow.

2. It must take this matter out of the hands of diplomats who, like their politician counterparts (both Palestinian and Israeli), have proven incapable of halting the violence and have a vested interest in seeing the game continue. No more 54-year-long meetings. Action.

3. We (the UN and America as the world's superpower) must let the world know that Israel is here to stay. We must declare Jerusalem and all of Israel and Palestine a demilitarized zone that will govern itself but be protected by the full force and might of the United Nations – no weapons of any kind, other than for a UN peacekeeping force. This territory must be considered "sacred" not just on religious grounds but on secular grounds as a place that was once in the "cradle of civilization" but has since become a breeding ground for hate, and emblematic of all that is wrong with humanity in the 21st Century.

4. While we are at it, as mentioned previously, why not a nuclear free Middle East, including Israel, plus a guarantee not to attack Iran or any other Middle Eastern country or try to change their regime, if they will abandon their unilateral nuclear program and support of undesirable organizations that promote terror in such a demilitarized environment? Israelis and American Jews can greatly contribute to this effort by being less partisan at the expense of the people who they illegally and immorally displaced.

5. It must create a sovereign Palestinian State, not a bantustan, based on a return of land seized in 1967. The key to dousing the fires of hatred and feeling cheated is to treat the Palestinians as well, financially, as we do the Israelis.

6. Thus, the future must be planned for NOW. The United Nations must provide the funds to build a Palestinian infrastructure that will permit the active pursuit of competitive commerce and a decent quality of life for its citizens. This must include a robust entrepreneurial and vocational training environment based on the adage, "If I feed you a fish, I will need to feed you tomorrow. If I teach you to fish, I will feed you for life" (AsimplePeace.org has a complete business plan for just such an entrepreneurial training and financing center). This infrastructure will likely cost less than the price to rebuild the New York World Trade Center.

Half-hearted attempts at this kind of solution have failed miserably. Referring to the concept of responsible parenthood, mentioned above, what has been done could be likened to a mother separating two children fighting over a prized toy. She gives one the toy and everything else he wants in life and shoves the other into a closet. You'd be angry too.

Instead of attacking Iraq and Iran economically and militarily, making their people suffer for the acts of despotic leaders who, like their Israeli and Palestinian counterparts, actually thrive on chaos and violence, we can defuse them by demilitarizing Israel-Palestine and making Iran, Iraq, Syria, etc., part of the peacekeeping force. Peace through INCLUSION, not exclusion can also preclude another Beirut Marine barracks disaster. It would be self-defeating to attack their own troops when they are defending their "brothers-in-the-faith."

In February of this year, Crown Prince Abdullah, Saudi Arabia's de facto ruler proposed that if Israel withdrew from all the occupied territories, including the Arab quarters of Jerusalem, then the Arab states would offer full normalization of relations.

His proposal was attacked by influential Arab leaders and scholars as one that "... will only confuse and weaken the stance by the Palestinians and the Arabs," said Wahid Abdel Maguid, vice president of Al Ahram Center for Strategic Studies in Cairo, adding that he worried that any attempt to appease Israel now might strengthen the political fortunes of Ariel Sharon, the Israeli prime minister. "Sharon will be the winner," Mr. Abdel Maguid added. "He would say `See, my oppression worked, and the biggest Arab countries are making unprecedented offers because of my policy.' "

This is no time for argument or debate; it is time for action. The world is at war with a global terror cell that draws its strength largely from its hatred of the Jews and America for 54-years of Palestinian suffering. The concept of compelling the two combatants to sit a table and talk to each other is a requisite, but only for the purpose of the UN telling them how the demilitarization process and transfer to a violence-free zone will be implemented and maintained.

The Ultimate Face-saving Solution: After 54 years, we know that the Israelis are NOT going to "do something to end their occupation." ASimplePeace's suggestion to forcibly separate two unruly combatants who have proven that they cannot settle differences that are now affecting the entire world provides the ultimate face-saving solution. If the United Nations (in the truest sense of the word) steps in and satisfies the 6 points listed in this White Paper, then we will be well on our way toward defusing radical violence throughout the world. The cost of such a venture is far less than what we all are paying on a daily basis. And no one will look the weaker.

Thus, the final piece to Crown Prince Abdullah's proposal is the creation of a "sacred ground" demilitarized zone that will be as untouchable and autonomous as Mecca or the Vatican.

The Palestinians have a lot of work to do in preparation for such an event. Before they can sit as equals at the peace table, the Palestinians must mount a major public relations campaign to reposition themselves on the world stage. Until the Palestinian people can rid themselves of their image as Keffiyeh-wearing masked "terrorists," they cannot hope to enter into a dialogue and demilitarization settlement that will have any chance of success in the court of world opinion. No one negotiates when one side is considered to be inferior to the other.

This public relations campaign must also educate the American public (including our U.S. Congress, many of who are too young to know what really happened in 1948, and have only 54-years of one-sided reports from the American press).

The Israeli Palestinian crisis is a major feeder of hatred of Jews and the United States on the part of radical Islamic fanatics the world over. We can continue to ignore them and they will continue to murder us (Jews, Muslims Hindus, Buddhists and Christians alike) both here and abroad.

ASimplePeace is working on the best means to implement the 6 points listed above, and invites your participation. Once we put out this urgent fire in the Middle East, we can commence a similar effort for citizens of other nations who have been subjected to the kind of injustice suffered by WWII era Jews and by the Palestinians."

Reprinted with permission from ASimplePeace.org, 2004.

We must face the fact that, as the literary editor of The New Republic, Leon Wieseltier, pointed out in a piece published in *The New York Times* Magazine ("Must Peace Wait for Democracy?" January 9, 2005), "One day between 2010 and 2015 there will be more Arabs than Jews between the Jordan River and the Mediterranean Sea." His premise being that the democratic January 2005 election in Palestine would not, by itself, guarantee peace with Israel. For example, Egypt has an autocratic leader, yet there is a peace – albeit a frosty one – with Israel. So, if democracy in Palestine will not ensure peace with Israel, what will? Many people believe that giving back what was taken from the Palestinians in 1948, and making financial (i.e. hard dollar) reparation, is what will ensure the peace. While this may be the simplest and most honest solution, mankind's greed, the power of the Jewish lobby, and the energy required to change the status quo make it an unrealistic one.

A more practical solution would be for the Israelis and all Zionist-oriented Jews to make the first move by admitting that their acceptance of stolen land in 1948 was wrong. If Pope John Paul could apologize for the Catholic Church's lack of backbone during the Holocaust, then certainly the Israeli leadership can step up and do the same for peace. This single act would deserve a Nobel Peace Prize. The Arabs and the rest of the world can join in this honor by publicly acknowledging that it is impractical to expect the

Jews to give back every bit of land taken under the guise of the humanitarian, but misguided, 1948 invasion, as well as the subsequent military "defensive" actions that further punished innocent Arabs for resisting their invaders. Then steps 1 through 6 of the plan proposed, what seems like so long ago, by **ASimplePeace.org** can proceed and quench the Palestinian people's more than half-century long thirst for justice and peace.

> **Defending the occupation has done to the American pro-Israel community what living as an occupier has done to Israel – muddied both its moral compass and its rational self-interest compass.**
> *Daniel Levy, Former Adviser to Prime Minister Ehud Barak*

CHAPTER 23

ISRAEL

All the world over, politicians and pundits are applauding Sharon's coming retreat. Yet a simple [Palestinian] lettuce-packer... seems to grasp what so many of them cannot: the lives of Gaza's Arabs will not be improved by expelling Gaza's Jews. *Jeff Jacoby*

A number of items in this chapter overlap with the previous chapter on Terrorism, and the one about Iraq that comes later, because they possess a common thread that can lead to peace in the Middle East and perhaps throughout the world.

Prior to submitting *ResoNation* for professional editing, several friends and close advisors (Jews and Christians alike) kindly reviewed it and commented. Their almost universal response to this particular chapter was that, despite the fact that I cautioned the reader at this book's very beginning that my statements and opinions are simply intended to provoke vigorous debate – i.e. to pull into the light of day things that many of us think but do not say for fear of seeming inflammatory or politically incorrect – they warned of the potential for vigorous denial and anger on the part of some factions for even suggesting that the Jewish people, and Israel in particular, could be both part of the problem and part of the solution to terrorism that is spreading like an "angel of death" around the globe. But, if we don't honestly and openly express these subsurface feelings and sensibilities how will we ever truly communicate; how can we expect to stop the loss of life and property to hatred and prejudice? Speaking personally for a moment, I will let my record of supporting Jewish causes, and my modest contributions to Jewish charities, evidence the goodwill with which this chapter is intended. Bottom line: if you don't like what you read here, then join the discussion and help set the record straight.

Rush Limbaugh, in a March 29, 2004 broadcast, claimed that the "terrorists are attacking us not for anything we've done wrong but because of who we are." But Rush's argument falls apart in light of the fact that, setting aside the attempt to influence the last major election in Spain, the "terrorists" are not attacking many other predominately Christian, capitalist, free-enterprise Western nations. They are attacking us and the British because, rather than doing what we know in our hearts to be right, we have permitted our foreign policy to be driven by Big Money, the military-industrial complex, and our almost blind allegiance to the most potent special interest group of all: Israel.

Our unconditional support for the Jewish state of Israel is deserved by a nation that has been a good friend to America. But to give that support in a manner that is needlessly detrimental and insulting to the Palestinian people – *i.e., giving Israel $3 Billion in aid, annually, and another "$3 Billion worth of military hardware, which it uses to pummel the Palestinians* – elicits feelings of disgust amongst citizens of even our staunchest allies. I say "citizens" of ally nations rather than their respective governments because, as it is in our country, Big Money and special interests control their leaders and elections as well. I am not advocating reducing our support for the Israelis in any way, but if we treated the Palestinians as well as we do the Israelis, and at no detriment to Israel, we could ameliorate a majority of the rage that is coming at us in dark, red waves of Christian, Jewish, and Islamic blood.

Israel and being Jewish (virtually indivisible subjects) are associated by the Islamic world as the root cause of the fanatic terrorism that is burning a swath of death and destruction across the globe. The solution to the two-headed problem of current-day Israel and centuries of Jewish persecution is intertwined in a painfully complicated matrix that involves multiple players with varied reasons for their respective actions.

We must never lose sight of how much the Jewish people have enriched our world: the inscription on the Statue of Liberty, one of the most recognized and revered symbols of freedom in America, was written by a Jew. The Torah (a Hebrew document that pre-dates current day Judaism) is the predecessor to the Christian Bible's Old and New Testaments. It gave us Moses, Job, Abraham, and the foundation for much of what we now refer to as "ethics and morality" in the form of the Talmud: the body of Jewish civil and ceremonial law and legend. The contributions of the Jewish people come from a 4,000-year passion for learning how all things fit with God and humanity. As one Jewish leader put it, *"Judaism is not a religion; it is a way of life."* But, ironically, that is a big part of the problem.

A RELIGION A RACE AND A CULTURE

The Jewish people are unlike any other people in the world because they define themselves as a religion, a race, and a culture. No matter where they live, or the color of their skin or hair, when confronted with a matter of national importance, there is an almost universal tendency among Jews to ask not only "is it good for the country in which we are living?" but also "is it good for all Jews?" This is true even for those Jews who do not agree with the Israeli government on many issues. This tightly interwoven, three-part identity accounts for the common perception that all Jews support the way the occupation of Palestine has been managed, and it is why we see swastikas and anti-Semitic slogans on placards at anti-occupation rallies throughout Europe. It is telling that many European Jews who oppose the war in Iraq say that they stayed away from protest rallies because of virulent anti-Israel sentiments among the protestors.

Many American Jews love secular America, but their millennial value system makes them feel more beholden to Israel. It is a testament to the memory of the Holocaust, as well as to the power of the Jewish lobby in the United States, that the moment one writes about such matters or even utters the word "Jew," politically correct alarm bells immediately go off. But the key to any successful relationship is open, frank, and respectful communication; that is the only way we will ever clear the air about opinions and feelings that are widely thought but seldom (if ever) actually voiced.

As stated in the message from AsimplePeace.org in the chapter on Terrorism, "Current-day Israel was formed as a result of an understandably sympathetic response to the torture and mass-murder of 6 million Jews – a horrific act that caused the world to overcompensate by taking the property of others so that the survivors of the Holocaust could have a safe place to live." But it is a smudge on history nonetheless as thousands of Arab families, who had lived in Palestine for years, were illegally evicted from their homes and farms by a misguided, politically motivated, U.S. and Great Britain. It is even more disturbing that the mindset that enabled this land to be pilfered continues to this day. Consider the following report, published in *Tikkun Magazine*, an Israeli publication that supports Israel while also advocating Palestinian rights; *Tikkun* conveyed commentary from the *Ha'aretz Editorial Board* ("An Israeli Act of Theft and State Stupidity," January 21, 2005):

> "[In July of 2004] Israel's cabinet adopted a decision that was neither made public nor even published in the official government gazette, Reshumot: to apply the Absentee Property Law to East Jerusalem, and thereby to confiscate thousands of dunams of land from owners who live in the West Bank. The reason for the decision was security-related: Since in practice, West Bank residents are barred from entering East Jerusalem because of the intifada, the cabinet decided to enact an official measure that would prevent any use of these lands by their owners in the future as well, and would explicitly state that henceforth their property belongs to the State of Israel. Even though the owners live only a short distance away from their confiscated property, their names and addresses are known and no one doubts their ownership, the cabinet decided to label them "absentees" and apply the law that enabled the state to take over refugees' lands when the state was founded, a law which has never been used since."

Fortunately, cooler heads prevailed. Under international pressure – the kind that the DayLight Movement will foster on a more consistent and reliable basis – Israel's Attorney General decided to repeal the government's decision to apply the Absentee Property Law to East Jerusalem and its plan to confiscate land from Palestinian owners without providing proper compensation.

CREATION OF A TAPROOT OF FANATICISM

Claims that Israel captured Palestinian lands in self-defense in 1967 are specious in light of the fact that that land, and more, was actually compromised, illegally, in 1948. Jews and Arabs were religious antagonists long before that travesty, but this single act fanned the flames of a hatred that gave root to the militant fanaticism that terrifies the world today. It was not always this way. For centuries, Jews were major trading partners and financial allies of the Muslim Arabs. The Muslims actually precluded Christian traders from certain valuable trade routes, which were then taken over, with tacit Muslim approval, by the Jews. Thus, it could be argued that the modern day hatred of Jews is more closely related to what happened in 1948 (see comments of Generals DeLong and Hoar in the chapter titled, "Terrorism"). To make matters worse, the United States, Britain, and the rest of the United Nations failed to adequately compensate the evictees after stripping them of their land and property; just like we failed to do for our American Indians when we formed our country – does anyone see a pattern here? In February of 2005, *Tikkun* asked:

> "There are grounds to wonder if the [recent] movement forward is more like the Oslo Accord, with huge expectations but no fundamental change of heart on either side, and hence no real change or follow through over time, leading eventually to the decline of hope. Are we facing another such cycle?
>
> The Palestinian people thought they were getting something far more generous when they agreed to the Israeli proposal of "Land for Peace" in the 1993 Oslo Accord. They were assured by negotiator Yossi Beilin that if they agreed to accept and live in peace with the Israeli state occupying 78% of pre-1947 Palestine, that Palestinians would then have a state of their own on the remaining 22% of land, encompassing all of the West Bank and Gaza. That agreement was refined by the Geneva Accord of 2003 which helped specify terms, including Israel giving part of its land near Gaza to Palestine in exchange for its ability to hold onto an equivalent amount of West Bank land so that some of the West Bank settlements could remain in place, and including a generous plan for compensation to Palestinians for their refugee status these past 58 years."

The Geneva Accord is the only peace proposal tabled that dealt in detail with all the grievances of the Palestinians in a fair and balanced manner. Yet the US administration shunned the authors of the team and would not formally meet them and consider their proposal. The US accepted Israel's allegation that they have no peace partner among the Palestinians. The reality is that the Palestinians also do not have a serious peace partner in Israel.

So far, all peace proposals have been nothing more than a public relations exercise aimed at trying to impose peace on the Palestinians. It is cynical and unrealistic to request a revolutionary freedom movement, whether Hamas or PLO, that has sworn to fight with all means available to recover their rights, to lay down their arms and make broad declarations that would undermine the very fundamentals of their movement in return for nothing more than a promise to start negotiations.

If Israel and the US, were serious about their Road Map for Peace initiative, they would have outlined, in detail, what the Palestinians would get in return for delivering or abiding by all the conditions necessary to get peace. The fight is about return of occupied land in *totality*; not about "percentages, water, compensation for confiscated private property, return of East Jerusalem, or freedom and right of return to one's homeland." All of these things are recognized rights according to international law. A vague promise to give the Palestinian people a state with no defined boundaries in return for dismantling the "raison d'être" of their organization is an insult to human intelligence.

Until the Oslo agreement, no Israeli government ever uttered the word "Palestinian," thereby denying the existence of a Palestinian identity – likewise, Hamas and the PLO denied the existence of Israel. Every Israeli government coalition has included a political party that either denied the existence of the Palestinian identity or their legitimate rights to statehood within the occupied land, yet their so-called "overture for peace" is accepted as legitimate. Ariel Sharon, "the man of peace," declared that two million Palestinians must be kicked out of the West Bank. He has never renounced this declaration nor has the US has asked him to withdraw it.

The Israeli-Palestinian peace negotiation charade is between adversaries who desire the total elimination of the other side. No peace negotiation starts with a publicly declared precondition that one side must renounce all of its entire original manifesto before the other side will show its hand, yet this is what Israel insists upon with tacit approval by the U.S.

The failure of the U.S, to encourage sincere negotiations and fair and humane treatment of the Palestinians is, as reported previously, further compounded by the fact that we send over $6 Billion in cash and armaments to Israel annually but a relative pittance to the Palestinians, who are forced to endure some of the worst living conditions in the world while awaiting justice for 58 years and counting. The Bush Administration's May 2005 announcement of a direct grant of $50 million to the new Palestinian Authority is obscene compared to what we lavish upon Israel. It borders on insult and, ironically, becomes just one more US-sponsored "good deed" that can be cast in a bad light by Arabs agitating for equitable treatment. Indeed, many pundits believe that this financial "insult" resulted in a steeling of resolve on the part of Palestinian voters, which contributed to the January 2006 victory by Hamas, a devoutly Islamist Palestinian organization.

How can a Palestinian individual realistically oppose what the world calls an unjust occupation by a U.S.-backed Israeli army that is willing to impose a ruthless set of living conditions to humiliate and crush any liberation movement? How would you fight against such a foe that took your home or killed your family? A friend who lived and worked in the Middle East, and who attended the Oslo Accord meeting, posed this question recently: "In light of the insincerity shown by the Israelis and Americans during the Oslo and Geneva Accord meetings, isn't the ultimate sacrifice of suicide missions, though hideous, perhaps their only option?"

Our leaders call Palestinian Arabs who want to fight for their land "terrorists," but we called our American Revolutionaries "patriots." We-the-People, Christians and Jews alike, would like to know what our leaders consider to be the difference. As offered in the chapter on Terrorism:

> **If it is to force their religion or ideology onto others, they are fanatics and terrorists. If they are trying to retrieve property, freedom, or rights that were unlawfully taken from them, if they are fighting against someone else's culture and values being imposed on them, then they are "defenders" or "patriots." That's how we differentiated them at the birth of our nation and it seems just as valid today.**

Many Americans are not aware of why we did what we did in 1948. As I see it, there were two reasons: (1) genuine caring and sympathy for holocaust survivors, and (2) votes. No one has used our Electoral College system to better advantage than the Jews. Because of their tendency to stay close to their own, combined with a desire to maintain their culture and bloodline, and because of prejudice (on both sides), those who immigrated to the United States tended to settle in closed, religiously defined, neighborhoods in large metropolitan areas on the East Coast. These cities happen to be in states that have a large percentage of our nation's total number of electoral votes.

There is nothing purposefully sinister about this electoral phenomenon. In fact if I were a member of a 4,000 year-old culture/religion/race that had not been treated very well over the centuries I, too, would want to band together with my fellow men and women for protection and advancement. Nonetheless, this mindset has resulted in a global perception that an inordinate degree of favoritism is being heaped on Israel by the US. What else should one think about a little country only 290 miles long and 85 miles at its widest point that receives almost a third of America's annual foreign aid budget? Accusations that such observations of favoritism are anti-Semitic are, at best, a knee-jerk reaction that has become standard operating procedure for closed-minded reactionaries. At worst, it shows a complete lack of intellectual integrity that, for 58 years, has done the cause of peace no good.

Israel does not exist just because its creation was "the right thing" to do. The will and hard work of the Jewish people is a primary reason it exists today, but it also exists because of the United States' sheer might and unwillingness to admit that the way it took land from the Palestinian people was immoral and illegal. Combine this with a fear of appearing to be prejudiced against the Jewish people (even though being Jewish and condoning the theft of Arab property are two distinctly different issues) and you have a solid shield of "political correctness" that prevents honest debate about how to remedy a situation that is becoming increasingly deadly.

"The moment the idea is admitted into society that property is not as sacred as the laws of God, and that there is not a force of law and public justice to protect it, anarchy and tyranny commence."
John Adams

In April of 2004, *Tikkun Magazine's* Rabbi Michael Lerner, opined about recent plans to withdraw from Gaza:

> "Perhaps the most extraordinary public relations gimmick in this entire charade between two militarists is the notion that Israel is "giving up" control over Gaza and thereby merits a concession by the United States. Unlike the West Bank where Israel can cite biblical ties and divine promises as additional motivators to its security concerns for continuing occupation, Gaza has been nearly universally recognized as a drain on Israel that provides exactly nothing for Israeli security or well being. Having kept the hundreds of thousands of Gazans in a state of penury and malnutrition that could only be rectified by U.N. aid, Israelis have long flirted with the idea of a unilateral withdrawal from the seething cauldron of hatred that its occupation managed to create. Yet Sharon's withdrawal will involve continued military presence in the south of Gaza, and along all of its borders-effectively turning it into one large Palestinian ghetto with no means of economic or political support."

NOT A PROBLEM; A SYMPTOM

The state of Israel is not a problem; it is a symptom. Its creation was intended to be both a remedy and an apology for man's intolerance and cruelty to those of the Jewish faith. The Jews needed a safe place that they could call home, but many people (Jew and Gentile alike) also say that the need for a distinctly Jewish state was also a consequence and a symptom of Jewish insularity, principled obduracy, and an ingrained attitude of superiority as "God's chosen people." Thus, it could be argued that, in both direct and indirect ways, the Jews bring many problems on themselves by cloaking their actions (good and bad) in an insistence that they alone are "God's chosen ones." For millennia they have purposely separated themselves in terms of their language, culture, and religion. Even in the late 20th century, Jews in many countries insisted upon having their own local government, courts, schools, and even their own charitable organizations.

To my Jewish friends I ask, "If the Jews really were 'God's chosen people,' would 'God's chosen people' permit the amount of strife and death that has resulted from the illegal seizure of Arab land and the forcible eviction of their fellow human beings? Wouldn't God's chosen people at least ensure that their Palestinian victims received fair and equal treatment for the past 58 years?"

If Jews do not want to be persecuted and discriminated against, they must do more to assimilate into the societies in which they live. This is a difficult observation to make about a people with so many valuable and generous contributors to their respective nations and to their respective communities, but that goodness is separate and distinct from a "standoffishness" that is sensed by their fellow citizens. For a person of the Jewish faith, this presents a particularly thorny dilemma in that people can adapt to, or even adopt, another culture but modifying one's deeply ingrained religious identity is quite another matter.

With respect to that mindset challenge, let us shine the light of reality on the term "God's chosen people:" it comes from the Old Testament, a book that was written by Jews. If anyone else even tried to take such literary and religious license, hypersensitive "PC" pundits would jump all over him or her. To the rest of the world a certain group's claim of being the "chosen ones," or of having rights to land that other's owned for centuries, sounds like another "David and Goliath" story or an American "Paul Bunyan" tale. People understand that great stories – especially those with a moral – need some kind of structural context for the telling and passing from generation to generation but "Paul Bunyan" stories provide a moral without requiring anyone to take them as fact or die for them. Bottom line: We are *all* God's chosen. To the Jews I offer this suggestion: "Be proud but less standoffish." The same can be said for many Muslims living in the United States, and for Christians who insist that their religion is "the only way." Practice and be proud of your faith but be "one of us," too.

To the Zionist arm of Judaism's credit, they got Israel reestablished after 1,900 years of struggle and oppression, which is a wonderful feat. But someone should remind those of the Jewish faith who exalt in this achievement, while also looking down their nose at Gentiles and Christianity, that it was two predominantly Gentile Christian nations that made it happen; albeit in a violent and unfair manner. Moreover, as mentioned earlier but is worth repeating, Israel is kept alive and safe to the tune of a $6 Billion annual "gift," from a predominately Christian U.S., the size of which far exceeds what would be given to any country relative to the proportionate percentage of citizens of a particular faith.

In editorial fairness, a more positive perspective on the value of the military portion of our "gift" was recently offered in an article published by *FLAME* ("Facts & Logic About the Middle East") a Website dedicated to providing a Jewish perspective on Israel and the Middle East conflict: "Gen. George Keagan, former head of U.S. Air Force Intelligence, stated publicly that 'Israel is worth five CIAs,' with regard to intelligence passed to our country. He also stated that the yearly $1.8 Billion [his understated number] that Israel received in military assistance was worth $50 to $60 Billion in intelligence, R&D savings, and Soviet weapons systems captured and transferred to the Pentagon."

RELIGION: A UNITER OR A DIVIDER?

The word "fanatic" has been used frequently throughout this book, principally in reference to Muslim "terrorists" or "freedom fighters," but it would be intellectually dishonest not to acknowledge that the term "fanaticism" can also be applied to Jews and Christians as well. In New York City, for example, on religious principle some Orthodox Jews refuse to move their illegally parked vehicles for snow removal on Saturdays. These are, by and large, good people who are fully conscious of the fact that they are not inviting goodwill or instilling favorable reputations with their fellow citizens. These misguided souls need to realize that they are right to place God first in their lives, but not to the point of imposing their religious beliefs into their fellow citizens' lives. This is about more than simple convenience: a blocked street could mean a fire truck or ambulance arrives too late to save lives. I hasten to add that this kind of behavior is by no means limited to those of the Jewish faith. Compared to the old Muslim and Christian practices of converting their fellow man by the sword, mere parking violations pale in comparison.

Maybe Christians do not do such things in a religious sense anymore, but they certainly try to shove their concept of democracy down the throats of sovereign nations that have their own cultural practices and traditions. While reported instances of Israeli "Gestapo" tactics against the Palestinians are certainly inflammatory, the Jews are not the only ones fanning the fires of hatred and anger in the Middle East. America's and its allies' military blunder into Iraq adds more fuel to the fiery hatred of Israel and of the Jewish people as a whole, regardless of their specific nationality (see the next chapter, *The Religious Right in World Affairs: Distorted Bully Pulpit).*

Centuries-old myths also add much fuel to that fire of hatred. Like most things in life, there is more to the subject of religious and cultural animosity than first meets the eye. Hitler, Stalin, and Mussolini were not the first to draw upon a 4,000-year pattern of anti-Semitic hatred as reason to blame the Jews for whatever was wrong in their society. Our Jewish brethren and we need to sit together at the DayLight Forum and determine why they have been persecuted by so many nations centuries before Hitler, Stalin, and even Christ were born. How much of this multi-millennial hatred has been brought on by the Jews themselves? The Jewish people need to look deeply inward – at their religious, political, and racial insularity, at their expressions of superiority and the acceptance of stolen land based upon biblical claims *that they themselves wrote.* A group simply cannot call themselves "a superior race" and not expect a reciprocal attitude of bigotry from those who they discriminate against.

> **"If you can trust yourself when all men doubt you, but make allowance for their doubting too ... you'll be a Man, my son!"**
> *Anonymous*

Certain Christian groups looking for a boost to their particular agendas have keyed in on the Jews. For centuries, the Jewish people have been savagely attacked for purportedly killing Christ; but, somehow, these ignorant Bible-thumpers conveniently miss a critically important point about our Jewish brothers and sisters: the Jews did not kill Christ. The death of Christ was part of a larger plan in which the Jews were important, but preordained, players. The Christian Bible's New Testament (John 10:17-18) clearly quotes Christ as saying the following:

> **"The Father [God] loves me because I lay my life down that I may have it back again. No one can kill me without my consent – I lay down my life voluntarily. For I have the right and power to lay it down when I want to and also the right and power to take it again. For the Father has given me this right."**

There would be no Christianity if Jesus Christ, a Jew, had not gone through the act of dying for our sins. There would be no "Christ" if He had not come from somewhere at some time. We can only conjecture that Jesus chose to come into the world in Judea and in the time of the Jews because, over centuries, the Jewish people had laid a strong and lasting religious foundation on which the Christian church could best be built. In other words, Christians owe a debt of gratitude to the Jews for providing such a foundation. Upon this foundation there had to exist a dynamic that would cause a schism; i.e., a time to "fly the nest." Like virtually every religious organization that has ever existed, with age and sophistication come complexity, formality, and ritual that create disagreement over what God really wants from us. For example: in Matthew chapter 15:11 and Mark chapter 7:15-16 Christ is reported to have uttered a statement that led to his eventual crucifixion as a heretic:

> **"You aren't made unholy by eating non-kosher food. It is what you say and think that makes you unclean."**

With regard to Christ's death, the Jews were "chosen" as a near-perfect counterpoint for Christian philosophy and nothing more. At the site of the crucifixion, the leader of the Sanhedrin (the highest court and council of the ancient Jewish nation at the time of Christ) is reported to have sincerely beseeched Christ to come down from the cross and save Himself if He were truly the Son of God. If Christ had done so, do you really think that Christianity as we know it today would have survived? It would have been reasonable to assume that Christ somehow survived His scourging and got Himself off the cross with an illusionists' conjuring trick, but Christ needed and *wanted* to die in order to rise again and be seen by both impartial and partial witnesses. Only an act as supernaturally dramatic as that could make an imprint on the world and on imperfect human minds – an imprint that would survive to the end of time, as we know it.

While we're on the subject of Christianity vis-à-vis the Jews, the next time that someone criticizes the Vatican for being silent during the Nazi atrocities of WWII ask them what their Rabbis were doing when the U.S. and Britain forced Palestinians off their land and out of their homes circa 1948.

As we look to the future, it is sobering to think that the world no longer views America as a leader; they view us as a bully controlled by money and special interests. The great majority of Americans, Asians, and Europeans feel that we are occupying the wrong territory. We should not have invaded Iraq; we should be devoting our maximum resources to cleaning up Israel-Palestine and the hurricane-ravaged Gulf Coast of our own nation. We cannot trust our politicians to solve the Israel/Middle East problem because they will never admit what we know to be the truth: for political reasons, we favor Jews over Muslims. Once again, a special interest group, in the form of the ubiquitous Israeli lobby, trumps reality while the rest of the world shakes its head in disgust.

As long as we continue to support our Israeli friends at the expense of the people who we helped to unlawfully displace, we will continue to fan the flames of fanaticism and terror. We may wish it was not this way, but that does not excuse us from having to do something about it. Only a direct democracy will be politically brave enough to vote to support Israel in a manner that entails equal treatment of the Palestinians. This is key to our safety and survival. If we leave it up to politicians, they will just continue to pander for votes and special interest money with the result being another 58 years of toxic hate, death, and destruction.

We can either make this relatively easy humanitarian decision now, or we can lose thousands more of our own people to escalating violence and fanatics who, because they cannot fight a conventional war against large armies, feel that they have no choice but to do as much damage to heavily populated areas as possible. Unless We-the-People act now, nuclear attacks are no longer far-fetched or far off.

As asserted in the chapter on "Religion and Spirituality:" Armageddon doesn't have to happen. Many people – Christians and non-Christians alike – respect the Bible, but also firmly believe that its pronouncements about things like Armageddon (which require man's action) are not absolutely inevitable if we exercise our God-given free will. Case in point: the biblical warning that "any nation that attacks Israel/Jerusalem will perish" can be precluded if we defend both Israel and Palestine in a fair and balanced manner. While it may be difficult for many Jews to accept the solutions to Israeli-Palestinian discord that are suggested here, if they really want to get their people safely through the 21st century, they need to face 21st century reality; they must work honestly and realistically toward a world that is safe for all of us. Under a referendum-oriented, direct democracy system, like the DayLight Movement proposes, many things about how we govern ourselves will change for the better. For example, without an Electoral College, Jewish lobbyists will not carry as much weight. Thus, all of us – Jew, Christian, and Muslim alike – will need to refocus our efforts and *work together* on realistic solutions rather than strong-arming politicians who will be largely eclipsed by active referendum participation.

The Jewish people will fare far better in the eyes of the world if they become part of the solution and live by their own words and precepts. The following quote from the Union Prayer Book (adapted) provided by Jessica Rosenblum, Assistant Director Brit Tzedek v'Shalom, the Jewish Alliance for Justice and Peace ("a national organization of American Jews deeply committed to Israel's well-being through the achievement of a negotiated settlement to the long-standing Israeli-Palestinian conflict"), illustrates this nicely:

> "As when we plant so when we reap… Help us to see that no work truly prospers unless it brings blessing to others' lives, and no gain truly enriches if it adds not to the happiness of others. Grant that we may never seek to dispossess others of what they have planted, nor build our joy on the misfortunes of our fellows. Help us so to live that when we shall have gathered our final harvest, many shall rise up and call us blessed."

Right-wing or left-wing, partisanship creates an evil dynamic wherever it is found. It is what permits the Israeli government to persecute the Palestinians. In the U.S., political radio hosts like Sean Hannity and Rush Limbaugh do their best to defend the Bush Administration's ham-handed attempt at spreading peace, security, and democracy around an increasingly hostile, anti-American globe. In a quest for listeners and advertising revenue, their misguided rhetoric is symptomatic of the kind of posturing that is dividing our country into warring camps on virtually every conceivable issue. Their actions are coming at a time when we all need to be talking in earnest about peace and survival, not about personalities and excuses to invade harmless nations. A national referendum system will preclude their demagoguery by pulling us back together as a nation – one with 300 million leaders.

A closing question: did the creation of Israel stop the hatred, prejudice toward, and persecution of, Jews or did it make things worse for Jews, Christians and Muslims alike? Ask the multi-denominational population of surviving families of 9/11.

I look forward to the day when there is nothing to write about Israel but positive news from Jerusalem as the seat of the world's three major religions. Repeating what I said earlier: Israel has the potential to help bring peace to the world but only if its leaders stop egging on violence and strife as a means to ensure that the United States continues to pay huge sums to "protect" it.

CHAPTER 24

THE RELIGIOUS RIGHT IN WORLD AFFAIRS

DISTORTED "BULLY PULPIT"

> **"Nearly half the U.S. Congress before the recent election – 231 legislators in total – more since the election – are backed by the religious right."** *Bill Moyers*

Lest it appear that I am singling out Israel as the *only* catalyst and flash point of terrorism, let's shine some DayLight on an aspect of the "Religious Right's" mindset and their contribution to a challenging and evermore dangerous world. While you might assume that this chapter would be in the "Domestic Policy" section of *ResoNation*, our country's Religious Right is exerting a profound affect on world affairs. In his seminal work, *The Left Hand of God* Rabbi Michael Lerner decries,

> "The unholy alliance of the political Right and Religious Right [that] threatens to generate a popular revulsion against God and religion by identifying them with militarism, ecological irresponsibility, fundamentalist antagonism to science and rational thought, and insensitivity to the needs of the poor and the powerless."

He goes on to assert that the Religious Right sees God as:

> "… the avenger, the big man in heaven who can be invoked to use violence to overcome those evil forces, either right now or in some future ultimate reckoning." [To the Religious Right] … the world is filled with constant dangers and the rational way to live is to dominate and control others before they dominate and control us'"

Actor, writer, philosopher, Herb Duval, put it this way:

> "Unlike some of their Christian counterparts, Jews do not proselytize. They may feel strongly that theirs is, 'the one true religion,' but they don't try to force it on anyone like Christians – especially evangelicals – have been doing since the Spanish Inquisition. To me, the evangelicals are the ones to be feared, because their goal seems to be to dominate." To me, the evangelicals the ones to be feared, because their goal seems to be to dominate."

That "we're always in the right" domination mindset, so heartily embraced by the neo-cons currently running our country, has caused us to recklessly plunge into a poorly conceived, even more poorly planned and executed anti-terror campaign that, in addition to being misdirected, has seriously damaged our reputation and relationships with both the free and non-free world alike. *The Left Hand of God* asserts that, "there are many very decent Americans who get attracted to the Religious Right because it is the only voice that they encounter that is willing to challenge the despiritualization of daily life, and to call for a life that is driven by a higher purpose than money."

For an antidote to this sociological paradigm Rabbi Lerner describes a desire among people for a more humane and sympathetic society that is not dependent upon decision making by politicians who are heavily influenced by Big Money, and whose "legitimacy [does not come] from a corporate-dominated media." He suggests that "A progressive movement or a Democratic Party that speaks to those desires in a genuine and spiritually deep way could win the popular support it needs to create a world of peace, social justice, ecological sanity, and human rights." That sounds remarkably close to the conflict-of-interest-free, direct democracy government proposed by the DayLight Movement.

CHAPTER 25

IRAQ

"Mission accomplished."
George W. Bush, 2,300 dead soldiers ago.

I am embarrassed for our country to have to give this paper tiger nation its own chapter, but Bush & Co., the military-industrial complex, and the way the State of Israel was formed have combined to foist Iraq into our lives. Even if everything that the Bush administration said was true – if Saddam Hussein had weapons of mass destruction and was harboring al Qaeda – it should have been the *world's* problem, not ours alone. Saddam tried to make a deal to stop our invasion of his country, but Bush would not hear of it. Why not?

The "Big Lie," a concept first voiced by Adolph Hitler, consists of "telling a lie so colossal that no one would believe anyone could have the impudence to distort the truth so infamously." The Bush administration, by refusing to admit that they knew Iraq did not have WMDs, has draped a false veil of validity over its invasion. As William Goldman, author of the film *All the President's Men*, said about Watergate twenty-five years ago, "follow the money." The reality of the situation is that we have an admitted draft dodger and former CEO of a leading member of the military-industrial complex, Halliburton, acting as de facto president and running the war decision process. Even Dwight D. Eisenhower, himself an Army General and the 34th President of the United States, warned against the danger of losing control of our country to what he termed "the military-industrial complex."

Attacking Iraq, the Bush administration has actually served the terrorists' purpose by distracting our focus and available resources away from al Qaeda, Afghanistan, and Osama bin Laden. Even our effort in Afghanistan and the pursuit of bin Laden are now being questioned as neither effective or the best use of our precious funds. Although we have been told that we are helping Afghanistan to become a 21st century democracy, in March of 2006 a man faced the death penalty for converting to Christianity from Islam. In a patently false attempt to save face after an international uproar the Afghanistan government backpedaled, claiming that the accused might be found "mentally incompetent" and, thus, not eligible to be put to death for his act. Does anyone doubt that, once this matter blows over, the Afghan government will commence killing non-Muslims over matters of faith? Is this the kind of culture and mindset that we should be fighting and dying for? Besides the avaricious pressure of the military-industrial complex, the primary reason why we are in Iraq and other third-world trouble spots is that our leaders do not know how to deal with the world's virtually universal anger and disgust over how we favor Israel over its Arab neighbors. In addition to being hated by the Islamic world, we are increasingly detested by our Western allies who we dragged, bullied, and shamed into invading Iraq with us.

> **"We must support our soldiers in Iraq because it's our fault they're risking their lives there. However, we should not bestow the mantle of heroism on all of them for simply being where we sent them. Most are victims, not heroes."** *Andy Rooney*

While writing this chapter, I spied a bumper sticker on the back of a BMW stating, "I support our President and our troops." The clueless owner has clearly confused two separate and distinct issues: support for George W. Bush, who got us into this mess, and support for the innocent soldiers who have no choice but to obey orders. In light of the irrefutable evidence that we were lied to about the need to invade a toothless dictatorship, one that was so well contained that its leader could not even fly over parts of his own country, how does support for our troops have anything to do with support for the dupe who needlessly placed them in mortal danger?

The ridiculously transparent spectacle of Secretary of Defense Donald Rumsfeld marching various Generals in front of the press corps to explain and defend a strategy over which they have no final say, is as demeaning to these career officers as it is useless. Do you really think that even one of them is going to take exception to our being in Iraq? Talk about a "career-ending decision!"

As soon as they leave the service, even Generals change their tune. In an essay published in *Time Magazine* (April 17, 2006 "Why Iraq Was a Mistake,") three-star Marine Corps General, Gregory Newbold, who resigned in protest as the military's top operations officer 4 months prior to the invasion Iraq, expressed regret that he did not more forcefully question our decision to invade Iraq:

> "My sincere view is that the commitment of our forces to this fight was done with a casualness and swagger that are the special province of those who have never had to execute these missions – or bury the results. Flaws in our civilians are one thing; the failure of the Pentagon's military leaders is quite another. Those are men who know the hard consequences of war but, with few exceptions, acted timidly when their voices urgently needed to be heard."

Generals live to fight wars, not to maintain stateside motor pools. Have you ever heard a general report anything other than the company line? We were "winning the war in Vietnam" right up to the time when we evacuated en masse. Those who deride comparisons between Iraq and Vietnam insult the basis of our human intelligence i.e. the ability to cross-reference, compare, and recognize essential similarities between separate events.

Those who insist that we must finish what we started in Iraq possess the same "loser mindset" of those who you see at the gambling table, going double-or-nothing again and again until they are completely destroyed financially; the difference here is that they are gambling with other people's lives, and with our money. Those who say that an immediate pullout would be a "disgrace" are principally correct. However, if there is no graceful way to win an unjust invasion or stop the unnecessary loss of American and Iraqi lives, I say *let us favor life.* The real disgrace was the greatest nation in the world failing to update its government to 21st century standards so that this kind of travesty could not occur in the first place.

The Iraqi people do not deserve to have us over there. They needed to have mustered the courage to take out their own despot, and only then invite us in to help them rebuild their country. Instead, we have wasted hundreds of billions of dollars that are sorely needed here at home for repairing America's decaying roads and bridges, for updating a dangerously antiquated air traffic control system, for educating our children, for keeping our loved ones healthy, and for accelerating the research and development of alternative sources of energy so that we do not have to continue the ruse that we are in the Middle East to promote democracy. Instead of wasting money on death and destruction, we need to shore up the crumbling physical and moral infrastructure of our own "shining city on the hill," which President Reagan so heartily espoused.

The usual argument put forward by the Bush administration and supporters of the Iraq war goes like this: "Isn't the world better off without Saddam than with?" Recognizing that Saddam was *not* an imminent threat to the US, couldn't we have taken our time and found alternative ways to get rid of him, even using clandestine and illegal means such as assassination, rather than rushing into a war that broke all international laws?

As mentioned previously, can you imagine the good and goodwill we could have generated if we had spent $1 Billion each on a bounty for Saddam Hussein and Osama bin Laden and even a fraction of the other $900 Billion on providing the Iraqi people with electricity, running water, and sewage treatment, rather than destroying their homes and infrastructure? Would that "bounty hunter" act have been worse for our international image than the way we are currently perceived? Can you imagine how infuriatingly insulting this has to be for the Palestinian people who receive, from us, about a tenth of what we have spent on Iraq in the last year?

For those who would argue, "Well, if the Iraqi people had taken Saddam out, he just would have been replaced by another bad actor." That's precisely the point and precisely why all of our efforts over there, all of our soldier's sacrifices, will be for naught within a very short time of our eventual exit.
For our next act, it looks like we plan to ask the Israelis to do our dirty work in Iran. You would think that the Bush-Cheney cabal would have learned from the debacle of Iraq and the less obvious, but equally serious, mistake in Afghanistan but now these madmen are starting their drumbeat for similar forced democratization of Iran, Lebanon, and Syria – and they are using Israel as our straw man. Does anyone smell Armageddon?

For solid evidence that we need a new way of choosing our leaders and making decisions, one need look no further than the Bush administration's ham-handed method of establishing a democratic vote in Iraq. In principle, the Iraqi election was admirable; in reality, voting when one does not know the candidates *names*, and when a significant segment of the population is not afforded even the opportunity to vote, made this just another Bush administration sham PR show. People need to *earn* the right to vote or they will not value or respect it. We on the other hand have paid the tab for them with the lives of over 2,700 of our soldiers who should not have died for this.

The best way to support our troops is not to put them in impossible (and illegal) situations. History does indeed repeat itself, as evidenced by the fact that "making the world free for democracy" was also the mantra of our leaders when they took us into Vietnam. In a 2003 speech at Harvard, former Secretary of Defense (and Vietnam war architect), Robert McNamara made a 40-years-too-late admission about our involvement in Vietnam that "we were wrong, terribly wrong" Triple-amputee, Vietnam veteran and former Congressman, Max Cleland, reportedly responded that McNamara's contrition "came too late." So much for the hubris of the "Best and Brightest's" claim that *"We know what's best for you better than you do."* For the Bush Administration it's proven to be easy to send others to their deaths in needless wars based on lies. In an October 2nd 2003 Op-Ed piece in *The New York Times* Cleland closed with a message to George W. Bush: "Welcome to Vietnam, Mr. President. Sorry you didn't go when you had the chance."

With over 2,700 American soldiers killed in Iraq, another 18,000 maimed or injured, and estimates ranging from 25,000 to 50,000 innocent Iraqi citizens (not soldiers or insurgents) killed, it's "more than a little late" once again. It's not that we don't learn from history, it's that our politician's motivation to learn is outweighed by their desire to do what they think will get them elected – i.e., pleasing the Military Industrial Complex who write big checks, and pandering to the Israel-oriented Jewish electoral vote – rather than what is right for our country. The DayLight direct democracy platform offered in this book will go a long way toward curing this kind of recurring tragedy.

> **[T]he leaders were spending most of their time, thought, and energy in trying to get into office, or in trying to stay there after they were in."** *Booker T. Washington*

Our parents, and now you and I, have abdicated our health, safety and financial future to Big Money and Special Interest Groups who do not always reflect our values or our needs. No parent would vote to send their son or daughter into needless combat but that is precisely what we have done in Vietnam and now Iraq. National referendums present a feasible alternative to our flawed decision-making process, especially when it comes to the protection of so many American lives at home and abroad. Appealing to our elected leaders has not worked. It is time to try something new – something that can disrupt the status quo without anarchy or further shock to America's already beleaguered system of commerce and governance.

STOP THE WAR BY BRINGING BACK THE DRAFT?

Recently a friend posed a question that really gave me pause: "If invading Iraq is so wrong, why aren't we seeing millions of protesters marching across America like there were during the Vietnam war era?" For a moment I was stuck for an answer until he wisely pointed out that the difference was we had a DRAFT back then. He then opined that, "Perhaps the best way to get us out of Iraq is for the Bush administration to reinstitute the draft. You'll see the truest poll when people think they or their loved ones, rather than strangers, are being called onto the killing field. This is the kind of question that we can raise at the DayLight Forum.

What we call "aiding democracy" in other countries, much of the rest of the world sees as America forcing its special interests onto the way a particular country conducts its sovereign affairs. If our reason for invading Iraq was to "spread democracy and freedom," then why did we not also attack Russia, China, or Saudi Arabia? We picked Iraq because of its oil, because it was weak, because Israel wanted us to, and because George W. wanted to play "cowboy" with respect to Saddam's purported desire to assassinate George HW. After the government's lies about the existence of weapons of mass destruction in Iraq, how many of us believe that this assassination plot was real?

Who are we to assume that a democracy like ours is the best form of government for a theocratic country like Iraq? A democratic Iraq will not stop the fanatics; fanatics will always exist. Our battle is not with the people of Iraq, but with the mindset of an ever-growing (thanks, in no small part, to us) fanatic fringe element of a theocratic culture. In our reckless rush to judgment, we overlooked alternative concepts, such as a monarchy. Why? Because, truth be told, we do not want strong leaders; we want governments that resemble ours as much as possible so that we can use the same Big Money pressure tactics that we exert on our own politicians. While I do not pretend to opine whether a monarchy would be a viable option, the concept seems to be more in keeping with the theocratic and monarchical history of the region.

The main reason that a large percentage of the world's Muslims want to kill us is not because they want to convert us; rather, it is because they think that we want to kill them. The 1948 Palestinian eviction and the recent killing of innocent Iraqi civilians certainly do not contradict their impression.

We should let primarily Muslim countries and their governments alone and allow them to be religion-based if they so desire – it is going to go that way eventually anyway. Middle Eastern culture is oriented toward *theocracy, not democracy, toward tribal infighting and intra-religion sectarianism, not unity.* It is simply a different social dynamic compared to what we know. Give them credit; they've done pretty well on their own for a few thousand years longer than our nation has existed. As asserted previously, most, if not all, of what we are doing in Iraq – all of the lives that have been lost or ruined – will be for naught within months of our departure. Describing the new Iraqi Constitution, an excerpt from *The Washington Post* ("War Supporters Concerned That 'Theocracy' Will Be Final Word in Iraq Saga," August 29, 2005) sums it up eloquently:

> "Islam is the official religion of the state and is a basic source of legislation,' the constitution reads, according to the Associated Press. 'No law can be passed that contradicts the undisputed principles of Islam.'
>
> Even though the constitution also demands that 'no law can be passed that contradicts the principles of democracy,' some in the United States who have typically supported the President's foreign policies worried that the outcome could be yet another Middle Eastern, pseudo-democracy that tramples on the rights of women and religious minorities, including Christians and Jews."

I refer you to the report, earlier in this chapter, of Afghan Christians facing the death penalty for converting from Islam.

"When the only tool you have is a hammer, you tend to see every problem as a nail." *Abraham Maslow*

The Bush Administration has done more to destroy our credibility than all others combined. We could at least forgive the Vietnam debacle as our "first mistake" but, as long as this one continues, it does not merit benign acceptance or forgetting. We-the-People must not permit those who perpetrated this travesty to remain in power. One murder makes a villain; tens of thousands makes a president – twice. How jaded we have become. I hate to say it, but maybe the loss of life on 9/11 was not enough to make us truly appreciate what we are doing to human life in Iraq and Palestine.

Somehow, al Qaeda's murder of 3,700 people is a travesty, but the Bush administration's using a "sledgehammer to kill a mosquito" and ending or ruining hundreds of thousands of lives (soldiers, their families, and innocent civilians) does not faze us.

Confirmed prisoner atrocities are yet another reason to get out of the Middle East. We have endangered any troops who may be stationed there, and we have endangered the American people for the next hundred years. If you think that is an exaggeration, just look at how hard the Palestinians have been fighting for the past half-century. How long will the fighting and suicide killings continue in Iraq? According to our experience in Israel, thus far, at least another half-century.

How is it that, as a nation, we can condone or rationalize our sins in places like Vietnam and Iraq, and in instances like the American Indian massacres and the internment of our fellow American citizens of Japanese heritage and the confiscation (theft) of their land during WWII, simply by saying, "despite all that, we're still the best country in the world," as if those cheap words can excuse that kind of behavior?

In a *New York Times* article ("Doing the President's Dirty Work," February 17, 2006), we learned that Senator Pat Roberts, chairman of the Senate Intelligence Committee continues to needlessly delay an investigative report on why George W. Bush *"...presented old, dubious and just plain wrong intelligence on Iraq as solid new proof that Saddam Hussein had weapons of mass destruction and was in league with Al Qaeda."* The article went on to describe how this same Senator is now, *" ... trying to stop an investigation into Mr. Bush's decision to allow the National Security Agency to eavesdrop on Americans without getting the warrants required by a 27-year-old federal law enacted to stop that sort of abuse.*

Mr. Roberts had promised to hold a committee vote yesterday on whether to investigate. But he canceled the vote, and then made two astonishing announcements. He said he was working with the White House on amending the 1978 law, the Foreign Intelligence Surveillance Act, to permit warrant-less spying. And then he suggested that such a change would eliminate the need for an inquiry."

In other words, if it's illegal just change the law and everything's OK. The American people deserve better than this.

Saddam is many despicable things but he was not an *international terrorist;* he was a puffed up despot well contained within his borders or at least within the confines of the Middle East. His "offer to pay $10,000 per martyr;"

Scud missile attacks; and praying in mosques were nothing more than cynical public relations ploys. The only time Saddam used WMDs (poison gas) outside Iraq was against the Iranians and we aided him with satellite photos and tacit approval or, at best, benign neglect. There is a definite double standard here: The Israelis have ignored or outright violated more than twice as many UN resolutions as has Iraq yet we invaded Iraq and deposed its leader. Pakistan, perhaps the least democratic nation in the world, has the bomb and, as has been widely reported, sold the technology to Iran, North Korea and Libya.

As stated in the chapter on "Terrorism," the Arab world and the Middle East admire our values as expressed in our Constitution but they are against us because our policies do not reflect those values. We need to be more consistent in matching our actions with our words. We may have had to do some expedient things during the cold war when there was another superpower but now that we alone are the most powerful nation and force on earth, we need to conduct ourselves with honor and set the example as world leader. We can start by telling the truth to the world and, first and foremost, to ourselves.

There is a moral civil war going on in America, between liberals and conservatives, over the Bush administration's biggest "Big Lie:" the existence of WMDs. As with most lies that grow over time this one has funneled our national conversation, about how to respond, into the same trap that forms our military leader's progress reports. Many of our political talk show hosts have gone from being forum leaders for active discussion to apologists for the partisan views of conflicted, often-corrupt politicians on both sides of the Congressional aisle.

It is very admirable that we live in a country where we can have forums hosted by well-spoken, powerfully persuasive, people like Rush Limbaugh and Sean Hannity on the right and Al Franken and Randi Rhodes on the left, but what about the great unrepresented rest of us – the American center – who want peace among ourselves and peace throughout the world? These talk show hosts are lending credibility to issues that are not as important as is bringing us back to a peaceful center. We should not be discussing how we got into Iraq or what our technique should be while we are over there; we never should have gone in the first place. We need to get out and never put our soldiers, our homeland, or our international credibility in such jeopardy ever again. Let this be the generation that stops the needless wars. Let the DayLight Movement be our rallying point.

CHAPTER 26

BEACONS OF TRUTH

In addition to heroically honest news programs like *The News Hour with Jim Lehrer*; Ted Koppel's discontinued presence on *ABC News Nightline*; and *Lou Dobb's Tonight*; two of our country's brightest beacons of truth are Bill Maher's *Real Time* and *The Daily Show* with Jon Stewart. Both of these *fake news programs* hold up a mirror of truth to the lies, conflict-of-interest, hubris, pomposity, and illogic that have so poisoned the collective American mind that a majority of us voted for George W. Bush to be leader of the free world – twice!

Maher's and Stewart's "truth squad" parodies and caricatures can only go so far. They're a nifty way of sugar coating a much-needed clarion call for change; a way to scream "fire!" without appearing to be a "Cassandra." Their guest segments open the door for real, not fake, change agents like this book and its proposed DayLight Movement and DayLight Forum. These devastatingly witty commentators provide an ongoing "wake-up call" about the propaganda and brainwashing that led us into Iraq. Propaganda that now threatens to tear holes in our Social Security safety net for the aged, the ill, and the widows and children left behind by hard working Americans whose income-earning years were sucked dry by needless military expenditures, the rape of corporate treasuries and corporate pension plans, and pork barrel thievery.

The reason that these news satire and discussion programs are so popular is the public's distaste for being manipulated. Two of literally countless examples are Bush's Department of Education bribing news journalists, like Armstrong Williams, to promote a particular government program, and putting out fake news releases without disclosing their source. In this administration, "the unbelievable is believable."

The night before Bush's second inauguration, I was speaking with two old friends who, like you, shared their insights and opinions candidly. Both are highly educated, spiritual men and died-in-the-wool Republicans. Shaking his head in wonderment over what he was about to say, one of them sheepishly volunteered that, in light of the needless deaths of thousands of Americans and Iraqi's, he would not shed a tear if both men were "taken out" during their inauguration. His companion countered with "It's better to fight them [i.e., the Iraqis] over there than over here." When I inquired as to when Iraq had attacked us or been proven to be about to attack us, my friend had no answer. I tried to let him off the hook by saying that I could see his point when we pursued Osama Bin Laden in Afghanistan but pride would not permit him to retreat from the same mindset that keeps our men and women in a no-win situation in Iraq – and, perhaps, soon Iran, Syria and the Philippines.

How is it that Congress and the press scrutinized President Clinton to the point of impeachment for a marital indiscretion, and John Kerry for what proved to be trumped up charges that he lied about his war exploits, but we *re-elect* to the highest office in the land someone who we knew, deep down, was sending our troops to die needlessly? Three words come to mind: "Halliburton," "fear" and "oil." Ask yourself whether our government and our supposedly all-knowing Central Intelligence Agency knew of the oil-for-food scandal long ago and conveniently pulled it out of their hat when Kofi Annan had the "temerity" to challenge our invasion of Iraq prior to the 2004 presidential election. Maybe Mr. Annan deserves all the bad press that he has received but it smacks of classic "Karl Rove character assassination" and distraction of the public mind to me.

CHAPTER 27

LIGHTS ON!

A charter Friend-of-DayLight member draws an interesting connection between the concepts of The Second Coming of Christ, the advent of the Internet age, and how the DayLight Movement fits in with all that is unfolding in the new millennium:

What if you read a prophecy that said, *"And behold, there will come a day when a new Sun will rise from the West and a new dawn for humanity will unfold?"*

Would you be excited about the literal thought of dual suns in our skies or would you dismiss the notion as an impossible metaphor? What if prophecy and Scripture were really intended to be understood metaphorically rather than literally? Before I elaborate on the creation of a new Sun from the West and what this has to do with The DayLight Movement, consider one of the oldest Christian prophecies – the Second Coming of Jesus Christ in the final hours of the world.

The New Age, written by B. F. Barrett in 1884, suggests that for almost 2,000 years most of humanity has misunderstood Scripture's concept of the Second Coming. Barrett suggests that the Second Coming has more to do with a literal awakening of the spirit in each and every one of us – a Christ-consciousness that will reconnect us to our Divine DNA. Barrett suggests that we started as spiritual beings who are now having human experiences and that the reuniting of our spirits while in our human form is what the true Second Coming is really all about.

Hmmm. Double hmmm.

Initially, due to my Judeo-Christian schooling, I was taken aback by Barrett's concept of the Second Coming being about spiritual growth and union rather than a literal reappearance. In an effort to understand Barrett's concept I offer my "Humpty Dumpty" concept: "Okay, what if God smashed his wholeness into a gazillion pieces, gave each one of us a piece (ala fractal hologram science) where each bit contains memory of the whole, and said,

"Go forth and let the game of growth begin. Let's see how long it takes you to put me (us) back together again." In my scenario the Second Coming would be a coming together, a spiritual reunion, of all of us rather than a "super-hero" Savior who swings down at the last minute and cleans up our mess for us, kicks butt, cleans house, we applaud; and "voila!" evil is defeated for a thousand years.

In this scenario each of us has a direct responsibility to play a part that cannot be delegated to a super-hero Messiah who appears in the final act. Each of us is either a part of the heavenly solution or a part of the hellish problem and this includes even those on autopilot who are not conscious of their part and responsibility.

I see The DayLight Movement being akin to Barrett's Second Coming – a call to action, to take responsibility, to tap our own individual beacons of light within, and to collectively and proactively engage in helping to bring about correction in the affairs of man around the world.

In essence, The DayLight Movement and ResoNation are about light – permitting darkness no place to hide; each of us willingly accepting the responsibility both for ourselves and our fellow man, to do our best, to use our best judgment, and to no longer delegate our free will to politicians who pretend to represent the "Highest Good." In other words, usher in a new world order based on complete transparency and light for all to see.

Now the funny thing about light is that it can spring from complete darkness. Witness the ancient Yin-Yang symbol whereby in the center of a complete field of white there is a speckle of black and, likewise, in the center of a complete field of black there is a speckle of white. These seemingly polar extremes perpetually spin in a dance of gravitational unity – a creative tension that holds the mystery of life together. In the density of that light there is a speck of evil and in the density of that darkness there is a speck of good. So, politically speaking, if the United States of America is an out-of-control, special interest-driven, spinning "black Yang," disconnected and misguided, then it stands to reason that somewhere in its center is a speck of white containing hope and seeds for change. Taking this a step further, if we employ our freewill and take positive action, we can effect this transition from dark to light, from "bad" to "good." I see the beginnings of the DayLight Forum being that speck of light.

Before Washington (in particular, the White House), was stolen from the American people and our global brotherhood of nations were betrayed, America led human history in two areas: capitalism and philanthropy. Never in the recorded history of man has there been a nation that developed so much material success and raised the standard of living so quickly for so many.

This point hit home when I interviewed social anthropologist, Howard Bloom (www.howardbloom.net). He described how, approximately 300 years ago, capitalism facilitated the transformation of cotton from "the Cloth of Kings, to an affordable fabric worn by virtually every person in the world, rich and poor, in cities as well as the remotest deserts, mountains and jungles. Prior to that it is estimated that the common man lost approximately 25 years of lifespan, because his clothes could not be easily washed. Perfect habitats for bacteria, bugs, and other unhealthy elements, pre-cotton clothing was simply unhealthy. On the other hand, royal garments made from cotton could be cleaned, were more breathable, and permitted freer movement, thus allowing the royal families to live longer and more comfortably than average folk.

And while the "Cloth of Kings," and many other societal benefits derived from the power of capitalism, cultural historian, David Walley opines that capitalism has been incorrectly linked to democracy, and this is why so many other global cultures have issues with the United States. E.g., China is modernizing but not "Westernizing." To assert otherwise would be to deny fifty centuries of heritage and being Chinese.

Looping back to prophecies and those that suggest, "A new Sun will rise from the West and a new dawn for humanity will unfold," what if these metaphors are not necessarily implying a literal new sun but rather a light that starts in the West in the form of the Internet?

When Barrett wrote *The New Age*, in 1884, he projected back another hundred-plus years to an eyewitness account of a "resolution in the heavens" that was witnessed in 1757 by scientist, philosopher and spiritual explorer, Emanuel Swedenborg. In essence, Barrett and Swedenborg claim that an event occurred in Heaven that rained down on mankind miracles of knowledge leading to radical discoveries in the fields of chemistry, electricity, geology, botany, zoology, and mathematics, that coalesced into a platform – a "springboard" – for even greater technical and societal development. The last miracle would be in the realm of human communications, the speed of which would create awesome powers to connect, thereby allowing humans to make up for lost time and for course-correcting and saving our planet and its inhabitants.

Consider the following paraphrased excerpts from Barrett's now 200-year old book and how close they come to suggesting that Internet communication – eventually linking all of us in a collective "Master Mind" – could bring us a giant step closer to celestial enlightenment:

> "The Dark Age built castles on the inaccessible peaks of mountains to fend off enemies; we build cottages on public Roads to facilitate access to each other. The Egyptians built pyramids over the dead; we build Roads to give life and swiftness to the living. The Chinese erected a wall to shut themselves in; we open Roads and ports and span the oceans with flying and floating bridges so that we may go everywhere and behold the coming of all people.
>
> What is particularly remarkable about all this 'road-building' is that it signified, for the first time in the history of mankind, when nations became demonstrably motivated to relate to each other; first in commerce and later in other aspects of culture and daily life. What is even more sublimely hopeful, all are feeling the positive pressure of great moral concepts like peace, liberty, education, religious light and unity. The desire for physical improvement of the land holds a natural and philosophic connection with all these great ideas, moral, and religious.
>
> The art by which the products of labor and thought, and the persons who labor and think, are transferred from place to place, is essential to social advancement. Without it no other form of art or commerce can progress. A people who do not possess this transference capability cannot be said to have emerged from barbarism. A people who have not made at least some advances with it, cannot rise above a low state of civilization. Nevertheless, this art has been, of all others, the latest to be perfected - so late, indeed, that future historians of social progress will record that its creation is one of the events that most eminently signalized our present age and generation."

But if human invention has been late in directing its powers to the art & science of transference, it has nobly compensated for that tardiness by an unprecedented rate of advancement once the concept of transference was brought into play. In the last hundred years, more has been accomplished in facilitating and expediting intercommunication, than was effected from the creation of the world to the middle of the last century.

Now, let's consider Barrett's quotes against the backdrop of prophecy handed down by Incan Elders. Reminder, these elders descend from people who lived in the mountains of Peru at 10,000 feet 500 years ago. When the Conquistadors started encroaching on their terrain, they migrated up to 14,000 feet and hid. Not heard from until they came down in the late 1960's, they pride themselves on being "keepers of the true prophecies." I met some of them at the Church of Saint John the Divine in New York City in the late 1990's when they were touring major US cities with a few cultural archaeologists from California.

The Incan Elders have a prophecy that says, "There will come a time when the Condor of the South flies with the Eagle of the North." I take this as a metaphor that the Condor and South represent people close to the land; natives who intuit the balance of nature and man on earth. The Eagle and North represent the industrial and technology-centric countries and peoples who have learned to harness science and industry but who have lost their connection to the land. Thus this "flying together" is, perhaps, a metaphor for the best of both worlds – one that is in touch with nature and also progressive.

The Hopi Indians have a similar prophecy and actually distill the struggles of "being between" the traditionalist vs. the progressive. I'll spare you the details of this other than to point out that Anglo-Europeans are the only culture that believes we were kicked out of the Garden of Eden – other native cultures have no such folklore. Thus, it is no wonder that in the 1600's Europeans debated whether animals and plants had spirits or whether other humans of color were truly human or savage beasts. If one believes fundamentally that we are separated from the Garden then, of course, there will be a "Them vs. Us" approach to life. But, if one understands that we never left and that our Garden of Eden is this very planet – a spinning, living, space station zooming through the galaxy—then one is better suited to take care of and respect all others.

In the book, *Sun Chief - The Autobiography of a Hopi Indian*, author Don "Sun Chief" Talayesva talks about his Vision Quests and how his guides advised him to travel the "Big Wide Road" and not get lost on an off-road terrain filled with cactuses, sickness, disease, lies and troubles. He was therefore advised to focus on the Sun in front and not the shadows along the way or off to the side.

There is something spiritual about focusing on the Sun and how the earliest or smallest light can dissolve human darkness. Stand in a pitch-black cave and light a simple candle. Its engulfing darkness cannot hide your candle's light. Light is nourishing and a catalyst for higher life – be it plant or animal.

And so, as The Daylight Forum proposes, let's get back to the original ideas of "We the People." Those ideas worked then and they can work now if we toss out the garbage of needless bureaucracy, corruption, and misguided policies that, as Toynbee wrote, have dragged down 19 of the last 22 great civilizations "when they reached the moral state America is in today."

Vote for referendums. Get informed. Think. Voice your opinions on the DayLight Forum "national heat map." Agree to disagree but let's focus on moving towards the Greatest Good for all.

I am reminded of the exhibit voiceover at what is now a national park, once considered sacred ground, on the Big Island of Hawaii. As visitors pushed the red button on the park exhibit, a native male voice spoke, "Even today, the age-old issues of men are still with us - how to use the earth wisely and how to get along with each other."

Accordingly, I invite you to join GregO's lead with The DayLight Movement and help usher in a new world that resonates with Light – especially when it comes to using the earth wisely and getting along with each other. Now it's your turn. Write your own thoughts, or even a chapter, about what you think will help advance the DayLight Movement and how we can make the world a better, safer, place. Send them to us at www.GoDayLight.org.

CHAPTER 28

CLOSE

"I would love to see politics be shaken up in a way that just completely blew out the ramparts of partisanship. That would be a wonderful situation." *John Stewart, August 2005*

In his book, *"The Trick to Money Is Having Some,"* author Stuart Wilde offered a sentiment that will apply to all who read *ResoNation* and then lend their support to the DayLight cause:

> "When the first human being began to write, he or she set the world upon a new evolution. Similarly, if a few individuals have the strength and the power to walk way from the restrictions of the world and to stand fearlessly beyond it, eventually in some distant millennium, all mankind will also come to that same liberation. It will be a special pleasure for you to look back, poised in some place in eternity, and know that you were there at the beginning of the movement. Your gift was that you realized at an early stage that you were indeed eternal, immortal, and infinite, and that you had the courage to walk with that idea in your heart while the rest of mankind said that such a limitless overview wasn't true or even possible."

As a reader of *ResoNation*, you are "at the beginning of the movement." In this age of global high-speed message dissemination, and with a push from people like you, we can accomplish its goals in our lifetime.

As stated at the very beginning of this book, the beauty of our mission is that, in order to succeed, the referendum-voting concept described herein does not necessarily have to become accepted. We will succeed simply by dragging important issues into the bright light of day, forcing politicians to declare whether they are in favor of open-book government and electing wisdom, and then ensuring that they follow through – forever. Let's see what happens to those who say "No."

I'll be looking for you at the DayLight Forum's Website and at various gatherings that the best of you will arrange. If we are fortunate, we'll even have our own talk-radio call-in program, which I am developing as you are reading this first DRAFT of what will be a perpetually evolving DayLight manifesto – one that you are welcome to help form.

None of this will happen without you and millions just like you. If I had "all the money in the world," I'd still require most of DayLight's financing to come from you, "We-the-People," because this is *your* movement – I just wrote up the first draft. DayLight will amount to nothing without true commitment and dedication from those who care about what the future can bring for all Americans. Note that I said, "*can* bring," not "will bring." We are no longer powerless and forced to accept what those who may not have our best interests at heart want to serve up.

I will leave you with a piece of advice that I live by and that has proven to be true from the very day that I embarked on the writing of this book:

PROVIDENCE

"Concerning all acts of initiative and creation there is one elementary truth the ignorance of which kills countless ideas and splendid plans; that is, the moment one definitely commits oneself, then Providence moves too. All sorts of things occur to help one that would otherwise not have occurred.

A whole stream of events issue from the decision, raising in one's favor all manner of unforeseen incidents and meetings and material assistance which no man could have dreamed would have come his way.

As Goethe said: 'Whatever you can do, or dream you can do, do it. Boldness has genius, power and magic in it. Begin it now.'"
W.H. Murray

Thanks for taking the time to consider and debate the purposely-provocative talking points offered throughout this book. Whether you agree or disagree with any or all of them, you're my heroes simply for entering the fray.
Gregory Olinyk
GO@GODayLight.org

Printed in the United States
148439LV00001B/1/A

9 781600 371356